BOUNCER'S GUIDE TO BARROOM BRAWLING

GUIDE TO

from: Nick

To : Katie

Merry Christmas

2022

This book is dedicated to my father, who has always understood me ("Son, all you give a damn about is your belly and your peter!") and who gave me sage council ("Son, the world doesn't owe you a living!"). Yet surely no children were ever blessed with a more loving, responsible, or supportive dad. Also, and equally, to my lovely and loving mother . . . the watchdog of his fury.

Next I must acknowledge my wife, Melissa, a strong and remarkable woman in so many ways indeed, as is certainly demanded to live with me.

Finally, to my long friend and fellow adventurer, Carlton Jackson, also known as "Quick Carl," The Kaliem. He left this life as he lived it—his back to a part of this world, taking council from few men and shit from none! Painfully, I shall ride with him no more in this life.

Perhaps, later on, we will share mead in Valhalla or dine on Golden Lamb in Paradise at the right hand of Allah!

A

BOUNCER'S

GUIDE TO

BARROOM

BRAWLING

Dealing with the Sucker Puncher, Streetfighter, and Ambusher

PALADIN PRESS
BOULDER, COLORADO

Also by Peyton Quinn

Advanced Combat Concepts and Techniques (video)
Barroom Brawling (video)
Blitzkrieg Attacks (video)
Defending against the Blade (video)
Real Fighting
Self-Defense against the Sucker Puncher (video)

A A Bouncer's Guide to Barroom Brawling:
Dealing with the Sucker Puncher, Streetfighter, and Ambusher
by Peyton Quinn

Copyright © 1990 by Peyton Quinn

ISBN 10: 0-87364-586-3
ISBN 13: 978-0-87364-586-7

Printed in the United States of America

Published by Paladin Press, a division of
Paladin Enterprises, Inc.,
Gunbarrel Tech Center
7077 Winchester Circle
Boulder, Colorado 80301 USA
+1.303.443.7250

Direct inquiries and/or orders to the above address.

PALADIN, PALADIN PRESS, and the "horse head" design
are trademarks belonging to Paladin Enterprises and
registered in United States Patent and Trademark Office.

Visit our Web site at www.paladin-press.com

Illustrations by Robert Stein, gnarlmaster aikidoist

CONTENTS

PREFACE

Training is useful, but it is no substitute for experience.

You didn't buy this book to read my memoirs, so I'll be brief about this. What qualifies me to write this book and then tell you: *If you read it carefully, practice the techniques, and do the drills with a training partner, you can significantly increase your odds against the guy trying to stomp you shitless or stick a shank in your guts.*

What qualifies me? In a word, *experience*. I am not referring so much to the more than twenty years I've spent in kwoons and dojos both studying and teaching martial arts. All that was useful, but most of what I am going to try to get across in this book is what my experience in real fights has taught me—in particular, what moves work and, equally important, what moves don't. This education did not come to me in a kwoon or dojo (in fact, it cannot be obtained there). What I am talking about here was derived from my experience as a bouncer in a rather rowdy biker bar, where I defended myself against dozens of attacks with fists, boots, pool cues, beer mugs, and, on four significant occasions, knives.

I don't claim to be a master of anything (except maybe riding my hog and having a good time with my scooter-trash pals). But what I put forth here are the techniques and attitudes for self-defense that I have used in real fights, not once or twice, but many times. Nothing works all the time, and anyone (I stress *anyone*) can get his ass stomped. The point is, I know that proper training in the applicable techniques, combined with correct combat attitude, can and will make the difference in an actual assault.

Just reading this book or watching my videotapes won't be worth a damn to you in a real fight. *You must practice to some level of proficiency!* I have chosen these moves out of hundreds I've learned in dojos because my instructing experience has taught me that the average person can learn them well enough to use them effectively in an actual fight. Also, I know from actual fighting experience that they work.

CHAPTER 1

THE AMBUSH
Awareness &
Avoidance

I have come to suspect that everyone who has done some real fighting arrives at some, if not all, of the following conclusions. The first and most obvious is that fighting is no game. It has serious legal and medical consequences. The second is that most of the time it is possible to avoid the fight. However, you must be willing to do so, and you must know how. This is the focus of Chapter 1.

Now, some of you are thinking, "I've heard this shit before. 'Stay out of fights.' I didn't buy this book to hear that. I bought it to learn how to fight better!" You might even be thinking about skipping ahead to some "techniques." If so, WAKE THE FUCK UP, PAL! Avoiding the fight *is* a goddamn technique, and not just a self-defense technique, either. It is an absolutely essential *survival* technique. It must be practiced just like you must practice a backfist or any other strike or counter covered in this book.

I said you have to be willing to avoid a fight, and you must know how. As far as the "being willing" part is concerned, some actual fighting experience works pretty well in helping you develop this attitude. Recognizing that many readers may not have this experience, however, I want you to consider a few things.

ESCALATION OF THE CONFLICT

There are a lot of people in prison, and a lot more in graveyards, because a barroom brawl or streetfight got "out of hand." I don't think those people in prison wanted to go there, and I don't think those people in the graveyard wanted to die. They went to prison or were killed because they did not think beyond some machismo bullshit they were sold at some point in their lives. The odds are good that there is someone reading this book right now who is working his way into prison but doesn't realize it yet. *Is this person you?*

If so, pal, give yourself a break. I have been in jail many times because of fights, but I have never been to prison. I don't want to go to prison, and I have a game plan to make sure I never go to prison. Having lived the life-style I have, and being a few months away from forty years of age, I think my "stay out of prison" plan has worked damn well. You see, I like riding my hog (the "Silver Serpent") on an open two-lane blacktop, making love to my wife, swilling down a brew here and there, and basically being a free man in America.

Are you interested in staying out of prison, too? If so, you must internalize your own "I'm not going to prison" strategy. Believe me, you do need such a strategy. Like I said, I have never been to prison so I do not know from experience, but I figure prison must be Hell on Earth. Do you want to go to Hell for a few years or maybe for life? If so, hold onto your machismo fantasies and play "tough guy" long enough and you will get there soon enough (unless the graveyard comes first). On the other hand, if you would like to stay out of prison, understand this—*either you are in control of yourself, or someone else is.*

Being in control of yourself is the first step to avoiding a fight. When you are in control of yourself, you are *aware*, and that allows you to make decisions for yourself, like, "Do I want to go to prison or maybe be killed?" These decisions are really pretty easy to make when *you* are the one making them and not someone else.

Depending on your life-style—where and with whom you hang out—you will get many invitations to prison, the graveyard, or maybe a lifetime hospital stay where you lie paralyzed with a bunch of tubes running in and out of your body to keep you "alive" for the next twenty years. You must recognize these invitations to such disasters, understand them, and decline them.

WHY FIGHTS OCCUR

Why do fights occur? If you give it some thought, you might come up with a number of reasons. But mostly it comes down to pride and ego—someone's insecurity and someone's pain. There was a point in my life when I asked myself, "Why the fuck have I been in so many fights? Why does this shit seem to happen to me? Why, when I am sitting in a crowded barroom, does somebody I've never even seen before walk up to me and, in the blink of an eye, whip out a shank and try to cut my throat?"

Now some of this just had to do with the life-style I pursued and the kind of low-life characters found in some of the places I'd go to. But I do not believe I have ever started a fight in my life (throwing a preemptive strike is not starting a fight, but we'll get into that later). So why was I in so many fights?

After a while, I could not tell myself that all these attacks were simply chance. It seemed to me that I had to be doing something that, at least in part, caused this shit to go down. But what? After all, these assaults seemed to come out of nowhere, totally without warning and for no reason. I began to look for clues by thinking back to all the circumstances that preceded the attacks. Well, I found those clues and, later in my life when I worked as a bouncer, I discovered even more clues that precede an attack.

One of the things I came to realize was that a lot of the blitzkrieg assaults I was subjected to were the result of my actually having too much fun. Sounds like twisted logic, but I know in my gut that it's true.

People who attack others in the bar or on the street do so because they are feeling pain. I'm talking about mental-anguish-type pain, not catching your fingers in the car door. This pain is carried around with them all the time, and it translates into aggressive or self-destructive behavior when the right cues appear. I like to enjoy myself and do so at every possible opportunity. My having such a conspicuously good time was the cue some of my attackers responded to when they attacked me.

Let's return to the aforementioned knife attack. That guy picked me out of all those people in the bar because I seemed to be having the most fun. When he looked at me, somewhere in that damaged psyche a little voice was saying, "Look at that shitball. He thinks he owns the world. He's not feeling pain like me. He doesn't know what pain really is. Well I'll show him what pain really is."

What could I have done to avoid this attack? I could have simply paid more attention to my surroundings. In other words, I could have developed the *awareness* to make observations and the knowledge to interpret them. Had I understood this at the time, I would have spotted that guy long before he ever launched his attack.

THE AMBUSH

A marine sergeant once remarked to me, "The enemy is best taken by ambush." Believe me, this guy knew whereof he spoke and was one of the toughest men I've ever met. (By the way, there is a world of difference between truly being "tough" and just being "mean.") The point is, the streetfighter—and especially the sucker puncher—also understands this maxim about the ambush.

The most likely attack you will encounter will come in the form of an ambush. The ambush requires the element of surprise. By being aware, you can eliminate this element, and without surprise, there is no ambush. This very often means that there is no fight. No fight means you, by being aware and in control of yourself, spotted another potential "invitation" to the aforementioned disasters (prison, graveyard, hospital) and were thus able to decline same. No fight means "you win."

When you win a fight in this way, you have defeated your enemy even more decisively than if you had pounded his face into raspberry jam. You see, this way you have defeated his spirit. You have held the mirror to his face and shown him his weakness. He really did not want to fight you—he wanted to ambush you. He was not confident enough to fight you any other way. He wanted it for free. In effect, your awareness told him, "It might not work out like you figured, dickhead, and any way it works out it's going to cost you some pain and injury."

A guy who is sizing you up for an ambush is acutely aware of your every move. Once he sees that you are aware, he knows his opportunity for the ambush is lost. Now the slime has to ask himself if he really wants to fight you. Most times, when he looks into that mirror you are holding in front of his face, he knows that he does not.

If I had been more aware, I could have spotted that knifer's intent long before he was on me with the blade. Chances are, if I had spotted him and made sure he knew I was aware of him, it would have been the only self-defense technique I needed.

Believe me, this is the best way to handle an ambush.

You must be observant and aware. This requires your being in control of yourself. Now let's examine this idea of "being in control of yourself."

AN ADOLESCENT STRATEGY

Before I learned better, I would sometimes spot somebody sizing me up, maybe thinking I was having "too much fun," and I would just want to get it over with. I knew that once the confrontation was past, I could go to a lower level of alertness, which makes it easier to have a good time.

I would walk directly over to the guy, making sure both my hands were in view. Then I would look him directly in the eye and, smiling all the time, I'd say something like, "Say, I notice you have been watching me pretty closely. I know I'm one hell of a good looking guy. You aren't a queer are you? I mean, is it that you like to suck dicks or what?" This kind of diplomacy got it over with alright, and real quick. Either the guy would start swinging right away or would be completely flabbergasted, as in didn't know whether to run, shit, or go blind.

Rarely, after his initial astonishment, the guy would just start laughing. This was always the most fun response for all parties concerned. If he laughed, I'd back off a bit with a remark like, "I was just trying to head off any bullshit hassles, man, or else just get 'em over with, but I can see you ain't afraid of me either." I would still keep his hands in sight, remaining alert for any possible attack, and I would not stay around long enough for him to change his mind.

Now consider the guy who started swinging immediately. He would not be in control of himself. I would be in control of him. It is not too difficult to avoid an attack that comes at your command, so the guy really wouldn't have much of a chance. It's just like standing there and saying, "I think I'm ready now. Let's see a right hook. Okay, go!" It was so easy, like pressing a button.

Now think—what are your "hot buttons"? What can make you automatically start swinging? Identify this shit and take these weapons out of your enemy's hands. Recognize attempts to control you and defeat them every time by being in control of yourself.

When I used this "do you like to suck dicks or what" tactic, it was sort of fun for awhile, but it likely did cause some unnecessary battles. Looking back on it, I was still allowing myself to be controlled by this adolescent idea of being "macho." Remember, you or I didn't think this macho shit up. Somebody sold it to us like they sell detergent or religion. Marc "Animal" MacYoung describes this little machismo game quite succinctly as, "My dick's bigger than your dick" in his book, *Cheap Shots, Ambushes, and Other Lessons* (available from Paladin Press and worth the reading).

When you realize this and transcend this macho mindset, you will have taken the first step into a larger world. It is a big step; that is why smaller men are unable to achieve it. I'm still constantly working on it myself.

GETTING DOWN TO CASES

I have a good friend, ~ ~ ~ I-- Reynolds. who said, "Give a lazy man a hard j
to do it." Working as a bo
and the easy way I found
hell of a lot easier to sto]
was to break it up once
spot an ambush coming
it happened. You, too, c
techniques. If you do, y
over most potential assai
The average saloon v
set up an ambush wit

beforehand. Unfortunately, reading these cues is primarily the result of experience, and it is quite difficult to communicate them in print. You must learn to spot them yourself. Keep in mind that it is not just one thing the guy does, it's a complex combination of body postures, eye movement, facial expressions, and so on. All these things add up to "ambush planning," and they identify the intended victim.

One of the things that saved my ass in the bar was continually scanning everyone around me. You can and must learn to do this on a subconscious level in such a way that nobody even notices you're doing it. This is the "see everything and see nothing" Zen concept. It means you never allow your full consciousness to settle on any one thing, but you are continually aware of everything.

The first and most important thing to scan is hands. When you can't see someone's hands, your alertness should go up a notch. They could be concealing a knife, stick, or gun. No shit, people, this awareness of hands has saved my life. It could save yours.

Another important piece of anatomy is the eyes. Learn to spot "hard eyes" from across the room. This is easier when those hard eyes are on someone besides yourself.

It can be very useful to watch a guy who does not think he is being watched, especially if he's hatching an ambush. Most of the time he really is pretty obvious about it. Also, you should see that somewhere in the toad's brain he is actually afraid. He may be working up his courage for the attack. Learn to smell fear and realize that your enemy will smell it on you.

Let me give you a typical scenario from my bouncer I'm walking down along the bar; most of the people ir backs to me, drinking. On my left are people at etimes there are people approaching the bar. my subconscious mind works in this ON 2 (second highest defense-condition kay. ATTENTION, rescan left; cannot see hands. Watch for possible weapon. Man has beer in other hand, face seems natural. Okay, hand now visible. On right, man turning body away from bar toward me, both hands visible. Weasel type on right, approaching bar, apparent intercept course. Pause and disturb his rhythm. ATTENTION, time to scan behind, no one approaching. ATTENTION, louder voices across room, possible harsh words. Scan, negative; only loud and boisterous behavior. No attack or ambush cues being displayed."

Get the idea? Remember, this is not paranoia. You don't have to engage negative thoughts in order to be alert. You do have to practice the technique, though. You can practice anywhere: at the job, while driving your car, in restaurants.

The most basic drill for developing this scanning capacity (which you eventually must develop to at least a near subconscious level) might be called, "Now what's changed?" You probably make some trip or walk past the same houses nearly every day. You also probably don't notice any changes in the surroundings, but actually it is really almost never exactly the same from one day to the next. Observe and note changes like: curtain open, curtain half open, curtain closed; light on, light off; car in driveway, car now parked further down driveway, no car in driveway, different car in driveway, second day car has not moved from driveway.

You get the idea. Someday one of these little observations might be critical to you. In any case, you are developing your awareness skills.

You can't avoid an ambush unless you can spot it coming. This is why you must develop the habits of the aware individual. When you are really aware, you see things more clearly and thus understand them more profoundly. You see the pointlessness of senseless conflicts like bar or streetfights. You also see that this nonsense is most often avoidable *if you have the will to avoid it*. Since there is no pussy in prison or the graveyard, you should find this will.

Now read that last paragraph again (kung-fu flute music in the background optional). I sincerely mean every word of it. I didn't start out in life with this knowledge—I had to pay for it. I paid a hell of a lot more than you did for this book, so take advantage of the bargain.

SOME FUNDAMENTAL ELEMENTS
OF AVOIDANCE TACTICS

As I pointed out, the ambush is the most common attack strategy, and simply noticing that the potential ambusher is eyeing you and letting him realize you've noticed often will defuse the attack. Sometimes, however, you will have to confront the ambusher more directly. Also, some dildos will actually test you out first for ambush potential. This may involve walking up to you (you don't know this guy; scan status is now DEFCON 3) and start running some verbal shit to see if you are a good punch-out prospect.

Again, I have no "works every time" tactic, but every strategy that did work for me had the following elements in common. Here are some points to consider for developing your own avoidance style.

Show No Fear
Communicate to the potential aggressor that you have no fear of him. This is best done nonverbally.

Example: I'm sitting at the kitchen table at a friend's party (scooter trash party). A stranger—pretty big, full biker costume, joint dangling from his lips—sits down in front of me and says, "I don't like you. I don't think you should be here." I look him directly in the eye, pluck the joint from his lips, take a hit, blow the smoke in his face, and respond, "Golly, I'm real sorry to hear that." I then give back the joint.

Sounds like a grade-B Hollywood movie, but that's

exactly what went down. My wife was sitting at the table with me and asked, "Why did he pick you? You were just sitting here."

I knew why because I was aware of my surroundings to the extent that I suspected some shithead might try that kind of stunt. You see, I was not wearing the right clothes for this guy—no cutoff denim jacket or leathers, Harley Davidson belt buckle, biker pins, and so on. Yet I seemed to be completely comfortable at this party anyway. This wasn't correct in this guy's universe. I was a "citizen," and citizens can't party with bikers. Again, I was having too much fun for this guy.

In sitting down like that and delivering his little speech, his cretin brain was thinking, "I'll make this guy uncomfortable." If he saw fear, he would have been assured that I was a good (meaning safe) prospect for a punch-out. Do you see that this is just another form of ambush? The biker was so worried that he might fuck with the wrong guy, he actually had to "interview" me first to see if it was safe to attack. Most of the time, all you have to do is handle the interview right.

Another way to make them realize you are not afraid is to play "crazy man." I've read where even the Apache Indians were afraid to fuck with crazy people. If a guy fucks with you, get some totally berserko look in your eye, breath real deliberately and deep, and say something like, "I know why they sent you. They think I won't recognize you because they changed your face, but I see it's you. They think I'm crazy and they can fool me but they can't." Then stand up, point at him, and shout to everyone around, "Look! He's back! They sent him again! They made him look different! But I know who he is!"

The times I've used this technique, the aggressors generally were totally fucking freaked and just wanted to get away from me. Sometimes some of my buddies who had seen my act before would laugh and almost give it away. You see I'm not really crazy . . . but I know who you are!

Project Confidence

This is similar to not showing fear but goes a little further. The objective is to make the guy realize that you are not afraid of him because you are entirely confident that if he attacks, he is the one who will get stomped. This is a little trickier than simply showing no fear and demands some imagination.

Example: I'm in this bar in New Mexico on an extended scooter tour of the Southwest, having a great time, when, being aware that I'm having such a good time, I spot some hard eyes on me. I would have just left, but I had arranged to meet a pal there so we could motor out to California and take Route 1 up the coast to Oregon. I was determined not to let this sleaze bag interfere with my trip. I knew if he tried to ambush me, at the least I'd be spending that night in jail as opposed to under the open desert sky looking forward to another great run with a tight bro. I decided I'd explain this to him.

Smiling, I walked over with my hands visible and sat down right across the table from him. "Do you know me, man?" I asked without any tone of aggression or confrontation, yet firmly so it was clear I expected a response. "No," he growled. "Who the fuck are you?" My response: "I am a person who tries to spot impending violence and avoid it. You see, violence can be a terrible thing." (Semivariation on the crazy man approach). "When my friends show up here, we plan on a nice cruise out of this little town." (I did not give any details of our itinerary that might allow him and any associates to relocate the ambush; I also deliberately implied more than one friend was about to show up.) I continued, "I hope I'm wrong, but I think you are planning to fuck with me. It could interfere with my plans if I went to jail because you forced me into some stupid little battle. You see, that would spoil my trip."

At this point the guy started getting vocally belligerent. Some people, including this guy, mistake being reasonable for weakness. I then told him that if he spoiled my trip, no matter what else happened, I would cut his balls off. He was wearing a knife on his belt; I was not. I added, "And you know what? I'll use your fucking knife to do it."

I had not intended to make a threat, as it's not really my style. But he made it necessary when he attempted to verbally berate me (sometimes called "woofing"). Few would have realized it, but his woofing was his way of working up his preparedness to attack (it's sort of like a long-distance interview). This is the "hot" portion of the interview. In telling him I would cut his balls off with his own knife, I had raised the stakes. In addition, he had to realize that I had noticed his blade and was not afraid of it or him. Further, my remarks suggested that friends of mine might arrive at any moment, again raising the stakes. Can you see why I failed his interview as an ambush candidate?

Now listen up. I don't think either of the above examples were situations I handled ideally, but they did prevent two fights by recognizing and defusing an ambush. Do not confront a person unless you are flat-out sure he intends to ambush you and you are convinced by the logic of the situation (not macho man thinking) that this is your best survival strategy. In both the cases above, that is how I felt at the time. But I realize that the second dude's attitude to some extent pushed one of my remaining "macho" buttons. Fuck it, nobody's perfect. But the next move, described below, is right on the money.

Alert the Proprietor

This is really important. If you spot a potential ambush, identify somebody who is an employee of the establishment. Ideally, this will be the doorman or bouncer, but the bartender will suffice. Inform this person that you think that the guy over there (clearly point him out) is trying to start a fight with you, that you have no desire to engage in any such bullshit, and ask if he could help.

Do not say anything like, "See that sack of shit over there? He's fucking with me, and if he puts a hand on me, I'll kill the son of a bitch!" First, you have just threatened to kill someone in this guy's establishment. This identifies you as a troublemaker. If you are talking to the bouncer, this is exactly what he is paid to prevent. Bouncers don't like people who make work for them.

Second, and potentially more important, your little machismo declaration has just provided the local assistant district attorney with a confession of premeditation. If you do have to fight this guy and he is killed, you have now bought yourself the more serious form of a homicide charge. Even if he's only seriously injured, when the police interview the employee that you made this statement to—and I guarantee you they will—his testimony will make the DA a lot more inclined to burn your ass for the hard fall. You know, as in "life in Hell" like we talked about earlier.

Give Your Potential Attacker an Honorable Escape

Don't do anything that's going to make the guy think, "I have to swing on this bastard now; otherwise he/they/I (choose any of the above) will think I'm a pussy." Give him a way out that does not humiliate him. Allow him to save face.

An obvious consideration here is that the guy is going to be a lot more sensitive about losing face if he is in earshot of his companions. In the examples above, the guys hassling me were apparently alone. Nobody could hear what we were saying. They also made me a little more angry (another face of fear, you see) than the person in the next example.

Example: Once I was faced with this guy standing by his pals selling me shit. I was passing through; they were locals, regulars at this bar. I suppose I will lay some more dime-store psychology on you now. No matter what the beef is, it's always something stupid and inconsequential. It's never really the insult, be it real or imagined; it's the mental pain that motivates these guys.

This guy was hassling me and spoiling my enjoyment because, you guessed it, I was having too much fun again. In this case, my magnificent scooter out there, packed down for an extended run, and my cavorting with the young nubiles pissed him off. He likely felt trapped, while he saw me as free. The guy was about one step away from a broken-down drunk, both physically and mentally. His buddies were in a little better shape, and I think they were waiting for this guy to push me too far so they could watch him get his ass stomped. I don't think they had any intention of helping him if a fight started. For my part, I was afraid he'd finally set hands on me and I'd lose my temper and blast him.

My tactic to this point was to ignore him, but he wasn't letting it go.

Finally, I turned, pointed my finger directly at him, and said, "You come here." I then walked back to a table away from his friends where nobody was sitting. I knew he'd have to follow me because all the others clearly heard my "challenge." If he didn't follow me over to that table, he risked being called a pussy in front of the others. (Once again, I hope you see how easy it is to control people who suffer from macho madness.)

I could see and smell his fear when he came over to the table. I was sitting; he remained standing. Basically, I told him that there were two ways we could work this out: he could continue his shit, in which case I would shortly begin banging his head against the bar edge, or he could agree to stop insulting me and I would agree to go over to his friends and tell them that I had apologized for my remark (an earlier, failed attempt to nip the guy's woofing in the bud). I explained to him that if he took me up on the apology offer and then uttered one more insult, I would be very cross. Briefly, I explained how I dealt with people who broke their deals with me and who made me very cross. (Again, we see a little of the crazy man strategy.)

He seemed somewhat incapable of speech, so I told him that I would take this to mean that he accepted my offer, reminding him, "Remember, if you break the deal . . ." and so forth. I then asked his name and he replied. I got up and walked over to the guys he'd been standing with.

When I got over to the other guys, I was a little surprised at what I perceived as their alertness level. They seemed to be at DEFCON 3. I told them that I was trying to avoid any hassles and that I wanted them to know that I had apologized to Russ for my earlier remark. I had planned on some words that would have let them know I was not to be fucked with (remember, some people will mistake being reasonable for weakness). I could see by their faces, however, that such remarks were unnecessary.

Russ kept his part of the deal. He got to feel macho or at least redeemed in front of "the guys." I was spared more of his verbal abuse, didn't have to pound him, and didn't have to deal with the consequences of same. As always, I informed the proprietor that I was trying to avoid trouble, but I did not tell him the details of the deal.

Now think about this. Why was I able to take this approach? Mostly because I was in control of myself and my potential opponent was not. But let's look a little deeper. I was more in control of myself than I might otherwise have been because this drunk represented no threat to me. It wasn't him I was worried about; it was me and what might happen if he set me off.

Suppose the guy had been some 6'4", 235-pound muscle man instead of a broken-down drunk? If so, I know it would have been a little harder to use my strategy. Why? Because he would be more likely to think *I* was a pussy! You should give these things some thought before you face one of these "whose dick's bigger" contests in the barroom. It will allow you to think more clearly.

Ultimately, you should see there is no logic to the machismo fantasy. Either you control it (and therefore others under its power) or it controls you, *and so will others*. Now read this paragraph again and try to make it sink in.

The previous example is an easy case for me to pick out because it happens to stick in my mind. This may sound a little crazy to some readers, but it made me feel good to handle the situation in that way. I felt empowered, like I was running the whole fucking show. Somehow I know there must be a level where even that feeling is transcended, but like I said, what the fuck, nobody's perfect.

Leaving your potential opponent an honorable exit must be achieved without violating any of the previous rules. This means you can't allow your creation of the honorable exit to be mistaken for fear. Neither can you allow it to be interpreted as a lack of confidence in your ability to injure your enemy. I'll say this again: these guys are like sharks. They smell fear like a shark smells blood in the ocean. Often, they will respond like that shark—by attacking.

Courage is not really the absence of fear. Think about it: without any fear, there really can't be any courage. Courage is feeling some measure of fear and then overcoming it, thus functioning as if there were no fear. Everybody has this courage in them. Remember *The Wizard of Oz*?

THE SEASONED WARRIOR

I don't claim to have mastered any of this shit, but I have not been in a real fight in years, and not from lack of opportunity or invitations. People cannot make me fight at their command. I will only fight when there is absolutely no way out. I like to believe that I cannot be made to fight over trifles, ego, false pride, or the like. Remember this concept because we will talk more about it later. All of the most dangerous fighters I have ever known (who were not psychos) have come to this same psychological position one way or another.

You want to avoid any physical hassles with these "most dangerous" people. Recognize when you are molesting such an individual. If you force him to it and leave him no way out (or he's given reason to believe he is in, or directly headed for, such a situation), then you will die. Do not make the fatal mistake of confusing this with an expression of machismo. It is not. Machismo is a false thing; this is a very real thing. Attacking such a person or his family or even posing to do so is an express ticket to the morgue. In the morgue, your corpse will lie on a cold, stainless-steel tray.

CHAPTER 2

THE REALITY OF FIGHTING

In Chapter 1 we discussed the concept of emotional pain as a motivation for assaults. Further, we tried to identify how this characterizes the ambusher's mentality. Understanding this, you can now appreciate the vital role of awareness techniques and how they permit you to avoid or defuse an ambush. Because of the consequences that can arise when "adults" come to blows, awareness and avoidance should be your first and most important self-defense strategy.

Your best strategy when someone is trying to pick a fight or set you up for an ambush is simply to leave. Again, do not confront people unless you are dead sure they are sizing you up for an attack. Also, only confront them when, for some legitimate reason that's not predicated on macho man thinking, you have decided that you won't or can't simply leave the premises.

PORTRAIT OF THE SUCKER PUNCHER

No strategy is perfect, however, and no sense of awareness is absolute. Consequently, we will now consider how to handle an attack once it is forced on you. The real basis for our techniques and defense strategies are predicated on a knowledge of how the sucker puncher or streetfighter most often attacks. In other words, *know your enemy.* Understand how he operates, his strong points, and his essential weaknesses that you must and can learn to exploit.

First, let's take a realistic look at the sucker puncher's strongest points.

Confidence

There is a first time for everything, but when you face the sucker puncher or streetfighter, it isn't likely to be the first time for him. He won't attack someone unless he has almost total confidence of victory. The sucker puncher by nature is not a courageous person, yet his confidence of victory is very high. Ironic, isn't it?

Keep in mind that confidence is essential for the effective execution of any technique in a real fight. This can be a shallow confidence, but the streetfighter has it going for him before going into the battle. If you aren't prepared, this can often be enough to establish his victory. After all, we have already established that his principal modus operandi is the ambush.

Now consider this. When a person attacks with no thought in his mind but victory, he is not thinking of technique or tactics. He is not even "thinking" about fighting. He is attacking. In a deeper sense, he "is" the attack. This concept is called *mushien,* or "no mind," in martial arts study. It is a fundamental Zen concept that refers to the state of mind whereby there is no delay between one's intentions and one's actions. With regards to self-defense and fighting, things like movement and defense become all but instantaneous. Martial artists will sometimes use meditation as a means to achieve this mental state.

Not having formal training, the streetfighter does not

know a lot of techniques or tactics, nor is he hindered by any compunctions about hurting people. Due to his confidence and spontaneity, however, the untrained fighter has *mushien* going for him naturally.

Experience
The streetfighter's confidence comes from experience. He's kicked ass before and figures that you will go down the same. If he had reason to suspect otherwise, he would not attack you in the first place. I hesitate to repeat myself, but again, do you see why awareness works?

There really is no substitute for actual fighting experience. The streetfighter has this experience. If you don't, it puts you at a fundamental disadvantage. Formal training may or may not make up for a lack of actual fighting experience. It primarily depends on the quality of your training, its appropriateness to actual fighting, and, perhaps even more importantly, your attitude, or "fighting spirit."

Competence
The streetfighter and sucker puncher generally have at least one or two striking techniques that they have mastered to some degree. These techniques are almost always either the right hook or the overhead right to the head. They have mastered one of these moves primarily through their application in previous punch-outs. In short, they have learned by doing. Once you really experience how to throw a good right hook or overhead right, you don't need much practice to maintain the ability (that is, at least as far as a barroom attack is concerned). This is especially true when someone employs these techniques from ambush.

Tactics
Many times, the simplest tactics are the best, and the sucker puncher's tactics are the simplest of all. He attacks

by surprise when his victim is unprepared to defend himself (definition of the ambush). He blasts him in the head (using one of the two aforementioned techniques) and never lets up on the attack.

Again, we have an irony here. The sucker puncher not only has confidence going for him and the previously mentioned Zen concept of *mushien*, but he also understands the importance of *continuous attack*. The result? Many times an otherwise decent martial artist never gets a chance to use his self-defense techniques against a sucker puncher's attack. Instead, he is blasted in the head before he knows he's in a fight, and then gets hit again and again until he drops to the floor. Once on the floor, he is the recipient of the most effective of all kicking techniques—kicking your man while he is down (preferably on his belly).

So what was lacking in our martial artist's bag of tricks? *Awareness!* (Say, maybe you have been paying attention.) He didn't have the knowledge of how the sucker puncher operates and thus the ability to spot the ambush before it was launched. I hope you are beginning to see why I dedicated all those pages in the previous chapter to the importance of awareness and avoidance.

We will return to the idea of how to spot and avoid an ambush. First, we need to establish some fundamental realities about how real fights work.

SOME CHARACTERISTICS OF REAL FIGHTS

Those readers who have been in real battles in the bar or on the street or have simply observed some punch-outs should try to recall what *really* happened or what they *really* saw in those fights. This exercise will help you grasp the fundamental point of these next few pages. You see, it isn't so much that the fight you were involved in or saw went down like that; the point is most real fights *are* like that.

For those readers without such experience, remember, I have seen literally dozens (it could actually be more than a hundred) real fistfights among "adults" determined to land that solid punch and put away their fellow combatant. Most of the time it goes down about the same. Here are the characteristics of real fights as I have observed them. The exceptions are few, though notable.

Real Fights Are Sloppy Affairs

Real fights are not like in the movies. In the movies, punches, kicks, and blocks are done very slowly in a prearranged sequence; that is, punch, block, counterpunch, etc. This is so the viewer can see the action, which creates drama. Drama requires some suspense—that is, one guy seems to be prevailing, then the other guy comes back. These shifts of domination are designed to create uncertainty about the victor (as far as possible, of course, since after all, the hero has to win).

There is almost never such back-and-forth action in a real fight. In fact, there is rarely any question about who will be the victor after about one-half to two seconds into the battle. Once a good shot is landed, it is immediately followed up by more such blows and the victim rarely is able to come back. Again, with the sucker puncher we see that if his opening strike connects solidly, then he repeats it, giving his victim little if any chance to recover.

Real fights are also much faster than fights on film. Have you ever watched a cat fight? All you see is a whirling blur of fur balls on the floor. You rarely can distinguish individual strikes by either of the feline combatants. Fights among humans are not quite as fast as cat fights, but it's almost as difficult to see what's really happening in any detail, especially without significant prior experience. The exceptions are when the combatants are real drunk, real slow, or real stupid.

After I'd experienced, observed, and studied my first

few dozen fistfights, I developed a better ability to follow the action. However, most times there really wasn't much action (that is, "technique" such as blocking and punching) to follow. Occasionally, one would see an attempt at a martial arts kick (which almost always identified the guy about to hit the floor) or some boxing moves. But for the most part, real fights are crude, sloppy affairs that show little if any martial study.

Understand that I observed this to be true even when I knew that one or the other combatants was a martial artist or boxer. In real fights, even people with significant formal training will often forget everything they ever learned and just go for it in a display of animalistic fury. They lose any consciousness of technique because they are consumed by their anger at having been struck and by their blood lust to injure their opponent.

Here we see another aspect of being in control of yourself. The fighter whose training and experience allows him to handle a real fight in a nonemotional, nonreactive manner while still investing his strikes with the emotional content of his fighting spirit has a tremendous advantage. This person's defense will reflect technique and training to a much greater extent. Most often, he will prevail over his assailant. But few people, regardless of training, ever are assaulted enough times to "get used to it" and not go animal. Consequently, one rarely sees much technique used in real fights.

You must learn to use the fury of the "beast within" to invest your strikes with power while still being in control of yourself. This allows you to use your best weapon—your brain—in the course of a fight. The beast by itself cannot use the higher brain functions and is incapable of any true reason.

Do not misunderstand what I am saying here. The reason people go animal when attacked is because it is the evolutionary survival mechanism that gives them the brute power, pain tolerance, and similar attributes to escape or overcome their assailant. To a large extent, this is affected by the introduction of adrenaline into the bloodstream. Surely this bit of biochemistry has saved many a man's life in combat situations, but this is not exclusively so. The adrenaline response is not always the best survival response precisely because it does affect, even prevent, rational thinking.

It is not an easy thing to accomplish, but the ideal situation is to be able to control yourself and your "use" of the adrenaline reaction and thus be able to use higher brain functions while dealing with a life-or-death situation. Though imperfectly applied, this is the real objective of military training techniques and discipline.

The legendary seventeenth-century sword saint of Japan, Miyamoto Musashi, summed up this concept as follows: "You must think neither of victory nor of yourself, but only of cutting and killing your enemy." Keep in mind that these guys did most of their fighting with razor sharp, three-foot-long pieces of steel that they practiced wielding almost religiously.

Old Musashi closed the medical record on a lot of swordsmen and spent the last few decades of his life in reflection and contemplation. At this time he wrote his book of strategy, entitled *A Book of Five Rings*. Written in 1645, it is still available from The Overlook Press, Woodstock, New York.

You should read this book. It somehow got popular a few years back and isn't hard to find anymore. Be forewarned: it is more than a little mystical and difficult for most people to grasp. However, if you have the actual combat experience necessary to form a frame of reference, Musashi's book becomes a transcendental masterpiece that you can read over and over and still discover something new, useful, and fundamentally significant.

Most Fights Last Only Two to Five Seconds

Actually, one could argue that real fights rarely last even that long. They generally are over very quickly, nearly as quickly as they begin. After all, once one guy is hit hard and rendered semiconscious, even though the other combatant may continue to beat on his head before the guy hits the floor to be stomped, the fight is really over after that first shot made contact.

One of the implications of this time frame is to underscore the fact that one does not really need to know many techniques for a real fight. How many techniques can you execute in two to five seconds? The answer is, not many. So you don't need to know a whole self-defense "system," but you do need to master a few essential techniques that are appropriate for actual fistfights and that can be applied to a wide range of attacks.

Most Fights Are Decided by Punches to the Head

Again, here is the sucker puncher's primary attack technique. Punching to the head is the mainstay of Western boxing, and for good reason. Of all the martial arts techniques I've studied, the single most effective striking technique is, without a doubt, hitting your opponent in the head with your hand.

Notice I said "hand," not "fist." This is because most people cannot hit the dense material that constitutes someone's skull with a closed fist with real force without sustaining injury to their own hand. This contradicts a lot of Hollywood action but it is absolutely true. Your hands were not designed by the Creator to take that kind of abuse. This is why boxers wear gloves. This is also why classical karate styles don't do much power punching with a closed fist to the opponent's head.

So how does our sucker puncher get away with his right hook or overhead right to the head? Primarily because he has a larger bone structure than his typical victim. If you have big bones you might get away with it, too, if you know how to land the blow correctly. The sucker puncher generally does know how to land the shot correctly; otherwise he would have busted bones in his hands every other time he punched someone in the head. If he stays at it long enough, he will eventually break bones in his hand anyway.

Listen, people, if you doubt this reality, consider the former heavyweight boxing champion of the world, Mike Tyson. Like all heavyweight boxers, he has a very large bone structure. Yet even Mr. Tyson broke a bone in his hand in a brief streetfight when a disgruntled "contender" swung on him. This incident occured when Mr. Tyson was coming out of a restaurant. Mr. Tyson did not wear his boxing gloves to dinner. If the heavyweight champion of the world (and surely one of the best fighters of all time when he trains hard and doesn't underestimate his opponent) can break his hand punching someone's head, so can you. To further prove the point, Muhammad Ali (in my opinion the greatest fighter of all time when in his prime) broke his hands more than once while fighting in the ring wearing gloves.

Later in this book, I will discuss how you can land an effective head shot and not break your hand. Naturally, these techniques are illegal in the sport of boxing. Nothing is illegal in a streetfight.

Most Real Fights Involve Some Form of Grappling

Even though a fight may not last more than five seconds and the outcome is generally decided in the first few seconds, grappling does occur. This is because even a semiconscious person will naturally try to grab the arms of the guy who is punching him in the head. The objective of grappling is to tie up the attacker's punching arms so he cannot easily land a full-force shot. The longer a fight lasts, the more important grappling becomes. In boxing matches, this is called the clinch.

A second aspect of grappling is when the fight "goes

to the mat," so to speak. A typical example is when the sucker puncher's head shot connects but either the power transfer wasn't solid enough (generally because it was partially or fully blocked) or the guy receiving the blow turned out to be a "hard head." (A hard head is someone who for whatever reason—thick skull, large head—cannot be easily knocked out by a blow to the head. All professional boxers are hard heads in comparison to the general population.) Since anyone can be dazed by a sufficiently powerful head shot, the hard head may be hurt and disoriented enough to preclude an immediate and effective counterattack, but he can and will grapple with his attacker to stop the blows for a moment. Then he will wrestle his attacker to the ground. What you have now is the classic "two guys rolling around on the floor trying to punch each other out." Most often, their punches while they are rolling around on the floor are not very effective.

If the fight gets to this stage (most involving a decent sucker puncher and the average victim don't), the outcome is a toss-up. Most sucker punchers and some streetfighters do not grapple very well, and their "mat work" is even weaker.

Personally, I hate to fight on the ground. For one thing, if the guy has any buddies or you have some enemies around, they will often start kicking your head and ribs while you're on the floor and otherwise preoccupied. For another thing, I was never particularly strong on mat work, either. It is the most exhausting form of fighting, and many times simple endurance will decide the outcome.

Grappling that leads to throws is another matter. Having studied judo for years, I will naturally throw an opponent who grabs ahold of me trying to tie up my arms. In fact, most of my real fights ended with some form of simple throw. Also, striking techniques alone on a guy who is considerably larger than you, even if properly executed, may not be enough to put him away. Striking techniques can set up a throw, however.

The throw generally is effective against a much larger opponent because his own body weight and/or inertia is used to collide him into things like: a) the pavement, which is real hard and unyielding; b) the edge of the bar, one of my all-time favorites; c) fixtures, like a fire hydrant, automobile bumper, or park bench; or d) the wall (brick walls are particularly effective).

Kicking, Particularly above the Waist, Is Not Very Effective in an Actual Fight

To put this more strongly, kicking is almost always a bad mistake in most fights. You want to keep your feet on the ground; this makes it a lot easier to "stay on your feet." Kicking is not only ineffective but actually exposes you to unnecessary risk against the sucker puncher or streetfighter.

Yes, I like to watch Chuck Norris films, too (haven't missed a one, Chuck). Kicks are used in films because they look great and identify the martial artist for the audience. You, however, must have no concern whatsoever for how you "look" in an actual fight. Your concern should exclusively be to defeat your enemy, not how pretty you look doing it. Remember what Musashi said. . . .

I didn't study various karate styles for all those years and not learn how to kick. But in a real fight, I leave most of the kicks in the dojo where they belong. The simple fact is that most people can't kick effectively anyway. Besides, hand techniques are both easier to learn and simpler to execute during the dynamics of a fight. Not only are they more effective, unlike kicks they don't leave you so severely exposed if they partially or completely fail.

The simple things you do hundreds of times every day, like picking up something or reaching for a doorknob, train your hand/eye coordination, which helps to make your hands more effective weapons. Your legs and feet normally only move you around, and that's exactly what they are good for in a fight, too. The legs move your weapons platform into effective range and to the proper angle of attack; this allows your hands to "fire" and damage your opponent.

There are a few simple kicks—none that go above the waist and most at foot or shin level—that are reasonably safe to execute in a fight and in certain circumstances can be effective. We will examine these, but the focus of our defenses will be hand techniques and simple throws.

The few times I had to fight someone for more than the aforementioned two to five seconds, it was either because the guy was simply real big and could soak up my shots or he had some higher level of training or experience over the average streetfighter. Naturally, this would concern me somewhat since most people who swung on me were dealt with right off the bat. But if the guy threw some kind of karate or kung-fu kick, I breathed easier because I knew I was pretty safe. Experienced streetfighters know not to try these kicks. It is only martial artists without enough real fighting experience that haven't discovered this.

SOME OBSERVATIONS ABOUT
MARTIAL ARTS VERSUS REAL FIGHTING

As I said at the outset, the techniques, attitudes, and approaches to self-defense put forth in this book are based on my experiences in real fights more than my formal martial arts training. But keep in mind that while my fighting experience is greater than most people's and certainly greater than most martial artists, it does not represent any kind of universal truth or complete understanding. What I am giving you in this book is what has worked for me in numerous violent confrontations as well as why I think these approaches and techniques served me so well. This demands that I point out why I've chosen these approaches and techniques over so many others that I have studied in kwoons and dojos across the country.

It is not my objective to challenge the combat utility of classical martial arts or any of the "new school" or nontraditional arts. For one thing, I didn't make up these moves myself. I learned them in martial arts schools and from individual instruction by some experienced fighters. Then I adapted them to work for me. In fact, every really good fighter I have known studied some martial art.

At the end of this book, I review most of the martial art systems that people study. Further, in light of personal experience, I make an attempt to identify their strong points as well as what I perceive to be their central weaknesses when applied to an actual self-defense encounter. I am sure there is something to offend everyone in my thumbnail sketches of these systems. My purpose in providing these opinions is to facilitate the reader's selection of a particular art for study in relation to his personal temperament, body type, and so on. (While I'm on this subject, understand that Western boxing is also a martial art and a very strong one.)

Remember, you cannot learn to defend yourself effectively by simply reading this or anyone else's books or watching my or anyone else's videotapes. You must train. You must have partners to train with and you must have some hands-on instruction by someone who is competent in a style. The martial arts school provides this.

In short, if you are serious about learning how to defend yourself, you are going to have to enroll in some martial arts program. To get the benefit from such instruction demands some level of persistence, dedication, and patience.

Listed below are some problems with classical martial arts training that I perceive will ineffectively prepare a student for actual fights. To derive the maximum self-defense benefit from martial arts study depends partially on your being able to separate what is art from what can be applied effectively in a real fight. It also depends on your staying with an art long enough to be introduced to its most effective techniques (seldom taught in the first year of study in most styles). It also takes at least a year and a half to three years to develop some level of competence in any system. I believe that once you have a good understanding of one system—and this usually means first-degree black belt—then you can pick out and learn the most effective techniques from other systems without studying those systems in complete detail.

In addition, the saying "forewarned is forearmed" is appropriate here. By presenting what I see as problems with classical study, it will help better prepare you to deal with some of the frustrations involved in such curriculums.

Asian Arts Are Predicated on the Assumption of a Lifetime Commitment to Their Study

Traditional martial arts training is deliberately slow and is designed to test one's patience. Even many martial arts instructors don't really understand this and believe this classical approach is the best or only way. Hence, they will say things like, "You must master these fundamentals before considering more advanced techniques."

There is some truth to this. However, martial arts were never intended to teach someone the most appropriate techniques for actual fights (as they occur today) in a minimum amount of time. Not hardly, to say the least. The training methods were, in part, designed to test a student's character before teaching him the really effective techniques of the given style. Patience was seen as an indication of character. People who quit in frustration had little patience and therefore shallow character. Thus the masters weeded them out before they learned too much. This was a way to avoid teaching techniques to a potential bully who would later abuse the local villagers. Such activity would reflect dishonorably on the master, as everyone would know the bully as the master's pupil.

While martial arts as taught in the good old USA have become somewhat less formal than their Asian counterparts, the basic curriculums of most karate and kung-fu styles reflect this original and fundamental concept of testing one's character by testing one's patience.

Martial Arts Are Concerned With Sport and/or Spirituality; Real Fighting Is Not a Sport and Isn't Very Spiritual, Either

I guess I could write an entire book on this topic alone, but I will spare you this and give it to you short and sweet.

There are no rules in a real fight. Yes, there are different levels of conflict. Most people involved in a fight are not really trying to kill the other person most of the time. But they aren't consciously or deliberately not using one technique or another because of some sense of "athletic contest" either. Karate and kung-fu sparring sessions and judo *randori* practice have very strict rules designed to prevent injury. In an actual fight, injury to the opponent is the precise objective. Since you are not allowed to use certain throws or strikes in most karate styles, the student does not learn to defend against such strikes very well, if at all.

In most martial arts sparring, the idea is to score one clean technique, thereby displaying that you have overcome the opponent's defense. Consequently, when one student lands a reverse punch, the match is stopped, the point is scored, and the opponents reset for the next round. Obviously this does not happen in a real fight. *Points are not punches!* One punch or kick rarely settles the outcome of a fight (unless it is the sucker punch from nowhere that puts out the victim's lights).

There is an even more serious problem with this training method. When two karateka spar, they are essentially "playing" at karate. Since both are usually of the same style and school, for the most part they both know the same moves. They discover that they can rarely, if ever, score with direct, basic techniques that carry real power. As a result, in order to score points and win matches, they work on tricky combinations that outwit the opponent's defenses to score the point. The problem is that, in almost all cases, these tactics are worse than useless in a real fight and generally very dangerous to try.

Just about all kicking techniques, including combinations of kicking techniques, fall into this category. I don't even think a superlative karateka like Chuck Norris would use a reverse spinning back kick in a real fight. Why the hell would he? He has an arsenal of simpler, more direct hand techniques and throws that would safely blast his attacker to the pavement. Besides, a person with Chuck's speed, talent, and total dedication to the art likely realizes that such techniques are for the movies and the dojo and are unwarranted and unnecessarily dangerous to employ in a real fight.

A second aspect of this no-real-contact style of martial training is that it often gives the student an unrealistic idea of the power of his blow. People don't go down nearly as easily as many martial arts students may think. Consider that people sometimes walk away from car crashes, gunshot wounds, and worse. A little slap in the face with your roundhouse kick is only likely to make your opponent angry, that is if he hasn't already pounded your lights out with an unglamorous straight punch to your head as your foot was recovering from the kick.

I know this to be true. Among other evidence, before I knew better (many years ago), it happened to me.

There was nothing wrong with my roundhouse kick to the guy's head, although I was wearing a tennis shoe rather than a hard shoe. These kicks just generally are not good energy-transfer blows like a well-focused hand strike can be.

Group Psychology and The Hawthorne Effect

Brace yourself, because we are going to get academic for a moment.

A few decades ago, a classic psychological experiment was conducted. This experiment took place in a factory, where the workers were divided into two groups. The first group was told that they were part of the experimental group and that the new lighting in their work area was designed to reduce eye strain and fatigue, which apparently was the cause of the many complaints of headaches from working under the old lighting system. The other group was told that they were the control group and would remain working under the old lighting system to allow an accurate assessment of the effects of the improved system.

The results? The experimental group reported all the benefits that the new lighting system was supposed to provide. In fact, their productivity increased as well. In contrast, the control group reported all the ills of working under the old system—eye strain, headaches, and so forth. As an astute reader, you have probably guessed that there was no "improved" lighting system. The point of the experiment was to see how people responded when they thought they were part of a special or elite group.

So what's my point? The point is, when you study a martial art, no matter which one it is, you will be immersed in a group that shares a common interest and you will be made to feel (verbally or nonverbally) that you are part of a special group. They study the "one true art" or practice under the "true master."

People will believe generally what they want to

believe, regardless of contradictory evidence. In a dojo or kwoon, you will not be exposed to much if any challenge to the practical application or content of the techniques you are studying. Everyone is there to learn the art, therefore they share and reinforce each other's belief in its power. They *want* to believe it works, so they *do* believe it works.

The practice of attacks and defenses becomes ritualized. The attacker cooperates with the defense so that, once again, the beauty, splendor, and wonder of the "True Way" can be elegantly demonstrated. Training ceases to become training in any meaningful sense. Instead it becomes yet another demonstration of the art in the laboratory of the dojo. All has been rehearsed many times before.

Now, dress everyone up in the same uniform—except for the high priests of the art; they wear black belts or black sashes—and guess what? You have both the significant trappings and psychodynamics of a cult! A cult does not operate on rational inquiry or individual and independent thinking. A cult operates on a belief and faith in some truth which cannot be questioned or tested. After you throw in some mystic hocus-pocus about "internal chi" or the "dynamic flow of the natural universe," then you really have crystalized some of the fundamental elements of a cult.

One of the results of this situation is that otherwise rational people are convinced that their study of the given art has placed them in a position whereby they can easily deal with the common streetfighter or thug who might assault them. Unfortunately, an actual fight is nothing like any dojo rehearsal. I once had a student who had been beat up in a streetfight enter my self-defense class. I will never forget his comment as to why his previous year and a half of karate study had not helped him against his attacker. He said, "He didn't make the right mistakes." Even writing this I can't help but laugh. Actually, there are more than a few levels of significant truth in this statement if you ponder it awhile.

The bottom line is that you are not ever likely to get a chance to use most of the techniques you study in a martial arts class against a real attacker. This is because he will not cooperate with your execution of the technique like your training partner will in the dojo. The fact is, since the attacker did not study in your dojo, he doesn't even know how to attack like that. This is why it is so valuable to develop techniques of defense that can be generalized to many forms of attack from any number of angles. A technique that requires your attacker to make some specific attack in order for it to work is likely of very little utility.

Be Suspicious of Techniques That Can Never Be Tested

Some martial arts rely heavily on dislocating joints, bone breaking, and so on. The problem here is that there is no way to really learn these techniques with confidence, since you can't practice them with any degree of power or to their conclusion. It's pretty tough to find people who will let you break their bones or dislocate their joints so you can perfect your technique. For the same reason, these moves can never be proved or disproved as effective. You can never be sure that they really will break bones or dislocate joints, and even if they can, how will you learn to execute them with confidence when you can't practice them?

Generally, these crippling or busting techniques demand that you apply focused force to a very specific area when your opponent has been manipulated into a specific position. Either of these is tough to accomplish with any consistency in real fight situations. To achieve both at the same instant in an actual battle is very unlikely.

Some styles that include the aforementioned techniques are akijutsu, aikido, and various arts that identify themselves with ninjutsu. Many, though not all, people claiming to be ninjutsu experts or masters are simply living in a fantasy world and couldn't defend themselves worth a damn against the average street thug. However, I have worked with a few people who were serious practitioners of the art. Perhaps what I was introduced to is only one style of ninjutsu, and thus may not be representative of the entire art. I don't know. But when these guys showed me their stuff (about the only ninjutsu people I ever met worth studying with), I saw that they put heavy emphasis on joint crippling, bone breaks, and tearing ligaments, then using pain compliance on the damaged area. These guys were practiced and fluid and knew their technique. Maybe, and I have to say maybe, they could make it work in a real fight.

But even if those guys could make it work, so what? They had studied for years and were reasonably talented. Ninjutsu was a big part of their lives and they practiced every day. Very few people will devote themselves to martial art study in this manner. Very few people will ever master these rather esoteric techniques well enough to use them in an actual fight, and this assumes that they will work in a real fight. Therefore, to my way of thinking, such techniques aren't of any value to most people.

I say again: be suspicious of techniques that can't be tested or really practiced or that demand the manipulation of your opponent into a specific position while you strike to a very specific area of the body. They will only expose you to unnecessary danger if you try them in a real fight. To make these techniques work in a real fight demands, at the least, very long, serious study and constant practice.

Things to Think about While
Studying a Martial Art in a Dojo

I have put forth these cautions about martial arts training as it applies to real self-defense situations so that you can better profit from such study. I will confess to some mixed emotions here because martial arts training has done a great deal for me on a number of levels besides just helping to keep my teeth in my head. These arts, simply as arts alone, are very worthy of study. In fact, I do not see how one can ever learn to be an effective fighter without such study, despite the criticisms I have expressed.

Now listen up. If you go into someone's dojo, show respect. Do not be an asshole who constantly challenges the instructor. You will get nothing of value from this. To learn anything of value, you must, for the most part, keep your mouth shut and pay close attention to what the instructor is saying and demonstrating.

I don't think you can't ever question a technique or approach, however. Questioning is the central means by which one learns. What I am saying is to do so in a courteous, respectful, and appropriate manner. Nonetheless, if you have not studied any other martial art for at least a year or two (and frankly, even if you have), and you have only studied the art in question for less than three or four months, then you have not been exposed to enough of the art to ask any critical questions, so don't.

When you do have questions or concerns about a given technique or approach, watch more advanced students practice the movement. Ask them to assist you (if the protocol of the school allows this person to offer such instruction). When you feel you understand at least how the technique is supposed to work, formulate your question. Then, privately ask the sensei (instructor) about your concern regarding the technique's actual self-defense application outside the dojo.

There are other things you should do when studying martial arts techniques to evaluate their potential effectiveness in real fights. Principal among these (and something you should do before asking your instructor as previously outlined) is to think how you would "spoil" the execution of the technique if it were applied on you for real. In doing so, try to realistically consider how an untrained fighter might be able to defeat the technique in the manner you have considered. More importantly, if the technique requires the attacker to do something in a specific way in order to present an opportunity to apply it, consider if the movement needs to be defeated at all.

Many times, the attacker simply has to make his attack in an amateurish, slow, and clumsy fashion for the martial art technique to work. You simply must not rely on this. People who are slow, clumsy, and inexperienced are not the ones who will usually assault you (unless they are drunk). The person who assaults you will most likely have experience, know what he's doing, and attack by surprise if you are not alert. Believe me, people, this is the reality of the situation.

CHAPTER 3

THE TOOL BOX

It is a lot more important to know how to effectively avoid being hit than it is to know how to hit effectively. After all, if your defense is perfect, you would never get hit, thus you would never get hurt, so how much would you need to know about hitting back?

Of course, no defense is perfect and, in fact, you almost certainly will be hit in real fights, even if you are the victor. So we must begin our study of physical technique. The strikes covered in this chapter are only a sampling of the many blows I have studied in the martial arts. I have selected these because I've discovered from actual fight experience that these blows, at least for me, were all that were really needed.

For a couple of reasons, I am going to present what I have found to be effective blows before engaging the more important topic of avoiding the strike. First, you must learn to make your avoidance of an incoming strike and your counterblow a single movement. By this I mean you should avoid any separation between slipping the opponent's shot and returning your own blow, as is represented by the concept of block, then strike. If you understand how to first make an effective strike, you will more easily understand how to achieve this unity of slipping the blow while simultaneously returning your own shot.

Second, the power of your blow will be amplified by the failure of your opponent's strike. In effect, you will use some of his power for your blow. To grasp this concept you must first understand the elements of a powerful blow and how to effect such a blow.

Think of the strikes I will put forth in this chapter simply as tools in your "tool box." Just because you have a fine set of tools does not indicate that you can build a house. Similarly, knowing how to execute these blows does not mean you know how to use them in a fight. We will discuss more deeply how these strikes are used in the dynamics of a fight when we study how to avoid being hit. It is not always possible to completely avoid an incoming blow, but our defensive tactics will be based on a strategy of at least breaking the blow's focus. This will keep you from being put out of the picture at the outset of an attack, thus allowing you the opportunity for a counterattack.

There are some fundamentals involved in the delivery of an effective blow that are true regardless of the particular strike. The most important of these is the concept of muscle relaxation prior to the blow's impact. This relaxation permits great speed.

THE THREE COMPONENTS OF SPEED

A number of people have the mistaken idea that a person's speed is a natural, immutable thing that is determined at conception, like black, white, or yellow skin. This is only partially true. Some people are naturally faster than others, but almost anyone can greatly improve their speed with proper training. I am referring to improving all of the components of speed as well as simply how fast your hand moves.

Speed is very important in fighting. I could say speed is everything in fighting, but this would likely mislead many people because most people think of speed as no more than how fast something moves. In the context of fighting, however, speed means a lot more than that and has a number of significant components.

Perception is the first component of speed. Remember my example when I asked the guy who was sizing me up for an ambush if he was a queer in order to force his strike or compel him to back off? In that situation, I was poised and alert for his blow. He could have been "faster" than me in one sense, but that wouldn't have helped him. I still would have defeated his strike because I was facing him, perceptually ready for his attack. Since my experience would have allowed me to see the strike coming long before it was truly formed and in full motion, it would have been pretty easy for me to intercept. If you think about it, you can see that the strike would basically have come at my command.

You, too, must learn to perceive body cues that precede the delivery of a blow from a person who is at rest. You can learn these cues to some extent from the "perception drills" I describe later in the book. For now, recognize that perceiving an opponent's intention to strike and the impending angle of attack is the first component of speed.

It may seem strange to people without enough fight experience, but once the blows are flying, perceiving both the intent to strike and the vector of the blow is not exclusively dependent on visual cues. Once the fight is engaged, it is shifts in body weight and the tactile feeling of your hands on your opponent's body that allow the experienced fighter to perceive the next blow. We will present drills to develop your abilities in this area.

The second component of speed is the time it takes

you, once you perceive the need for a given action, to actually execute that action. This is simple enough. You see the guy begin to form a fist as his punching-side shoulder begins to drop and you perceive the intent of a right hook to your head. Now you must react. This means you must choose a response and execute same.

Obviously, there is no time for you to think, "Hmm, looks like the right hook alright. Should I go for a rising block? Or how about a slap block?" By that time the blow will have connected and put you away. You must react immediately without, or at least with a minimum of, conscious thought. The first thing we will do to decrease your reaction time is reduce your choices of response to the absolute minimum. This is why I will present only two basic methods to slip a blow. If properly applied, these two methods will be effective against almost every type of strike.

Note that, philosophically, this is directly opposed to most martial arts systems that try to teach a variety of techniques to block a variety of punches or attacks. This is simply unnecessary for most real fighting. Further, reliance on a variety of techniques can confuse the mind—that is, it can divide the defender's consciousness and place a barrier between the enemy's attack and the defender's response. My method tends to eliminate this problem.

Finally, there's the third component of speed. You have perceived the attack and thus the need to respond, your brain has selected the response (all of which occurs in a fraction of a second); now we are down to what most people consider speed, that is, how fast something moves.

The chief deterent to how fast you move is how much you slow yourself down. You slow yourself down by placing muscular tension in your limb before you strike. Tension in your muscles causes friction and resistance to movement, which you must then overcome to deliver the blow. This tension is a reflection of tension in your mind.

You can learn to control your mind and thus your speed.

Before proceeding, how about a colorful story to illustrate the point? This is a trick I have used in bars to win a few drinks or other saloon wagers and, on one occasion, to convince a guy that he did not want to fight me. It is simple to learn, helps you understand how fast movement is achieved, and provides a good example of how all the aforementioned components of speed work in unison. Most observers won't or can't differentiate the components of speed, so to them, this trick just seems like, "Jesus, that fucker is quick!" Yet I think almost anybody can learn to double their speed and most anyone can learn this coin trick, too. Here's the deal.

I would have the guy stretch out his palm facing up. Then I would place a coin in the center of his palm and step back slightly. I would tell him to look at that coin because I was going to take it out of his hand before he could do anything about it. Generally, the guy's response was, "That's impossible!" especially if he thought he was quick. If you are playing the game as a bet, this is when you offer to set the amount and odds of the wager.

You can only learn this trick by first learning to relax your mind and body so that your hand can move unencumbered by resistance. The speed and focus drills I present later in this chapter will help you develop this relaxation. In fact, the ability to relax is a key to success in many forms of sport, not just combat.

Because my hand was completely relaxed, as was my mind, I could move it very fast. This is simple, but you must experience it through the drills. It is one of those things where the first time you do it right, then you understand the truth of it. Once you've done it successfully, try to repeat it, but beware! If you are concerned about "doing it right again," you will reintroduce tension and fail. Old Musashi's caution, "Think neither of victory nor of yourself . . ." will have new and more profound meaning once you do this trick correctly.

I once pulled this stunt to discourage a guy who was "interviewing" me as a punch-out prospect. After I snatched the coin from his hand, he stood staring in disbelief at his empty palm. That's when I asked him if we couldn't try to get along better because if he fucked with me, I'd have to snatch one of his eyes out of his head the same way. The fucker was convinced.

Actually, I don't think I could snatch an eye out of someone's head, but he didn't know that.

Before leaving this coin-trick subject, there are some other reasons why I brought it up. By having the guy look at the coin, I deprived him of looking at my body and thus any physical cues I might have given that would precede my movement. I didn't give many, if any, such cues. In any case, by looking at the coin, the first component of speed—perception—was denied him. Second, even if the guy was real fast, when my hand entered his outstretched palm, he was physically prevented from closing it the instant I snatched the coin. When my hand slapped onto his palm, it bounced the coin up into my palm. Since I initiated the movement, I was perceptually ready to catch the coin and withdraw my hand in one movement.

Now, since the guy had never experienced such a thing before and his mind was not perceptually ready to accept it, he never realized that he was able to respond to any degree whatever. All he thought was, "*Bam!* It just happened."

In the above two paragraphs, I mention some reasons why the coin trick works. Some have to do with "concept," others with "technique." Read the paragraph again and separate the concepts from the techniques. Yes, I'm asking you to think.

If you study fighting long and seriously enough, and you have sufficient fight experience (and it doesn't always have to be a lot), you will ultimately come to see that concepts are more important than techniques. Concepts, once mastered, can be generalized to many situations, even beyond attack situations, but techniques are more specific. Concepts are strategy; techniques are tactics.

The conceptual elements of speed apply both to your delivery of the blow and avoiding the opponent's shot. In both cases, the success of your actions will depend on your speed as appreciated in all its components.

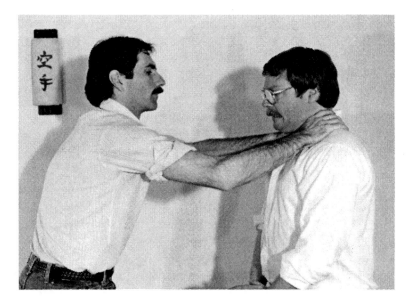

This particular sequence is offered because it provides a visual basis in which to appreciate the concepts of a) not contesting the opponent's power, b) economy of movement, and c) continuous attack. In this first photo, the attacker closes the distance with the defender with a front choke. The defender immediately senses the possibility of the knee strike to his groin and has already stepped back slightly. His hands drop, palms down, to defend against the possible groin strike.

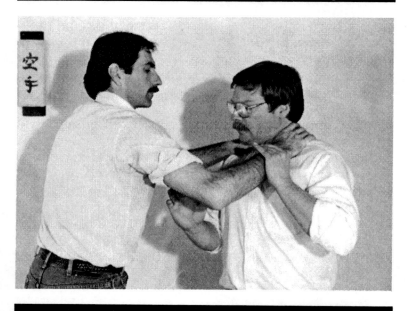

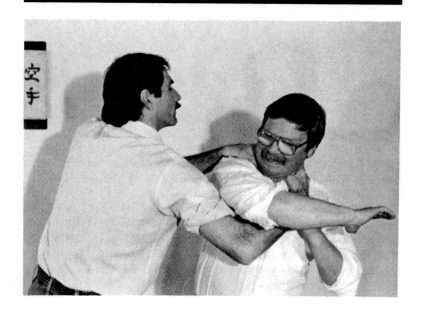

About a quarter of a second later, the defender captures the attacker's right wrist with his left hand (top left). This is done only to hold the attacker's hand in place and for tactile feedback, not to try to remove it. With his hands on the attacker's body, the defender now can sense the hand movements and shifts of weight that precede other attacks. Notice that the defender's right hand has begun to move between the attacker's two arms. The defender twists his body with this motion, which chambers the forthcoming elbow strike.

Notice that the opponent's power has not been contested at all to this point (bottom left). This leaves the attacker's hands in their original position at the defender's throat, making them unavailable to block the elbow strike. Also, since the attacker still has his initial throat grip, he feels everything is still going according to plan and is thus totally unprepared for the elbow strike.

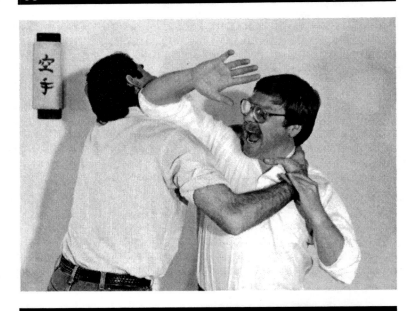

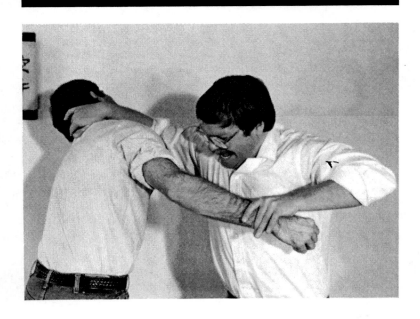

Bammo! The elbow strike connects (top left). It carries the defender's entire body weight because of the essential hip rotation that chambered this blow, as seen in the previous two photos. Note that the defender maintains his hold on the opponent's right wrist. If the attacker breaks away or frees this hand for a blow, the defender knows immediately and can counter appropriately. A powerful blow like this elbow strike makes the attacker see the little purple points of light against the black background.

The instant after impact, the defender rotates his wrist to change his grip on the attacker's wrist as the elbow blow becomes a grab behind the neck (bottom left). Note how the defender's right hand, already in motion from the elbow strike, was naturally set up for the grab behind the neck. This is an example of economy of movement. Observe the position of the defender's hands on the attacker's body; the leverage achieved on an already stunned opponent sets up the neck/wrist spinout.

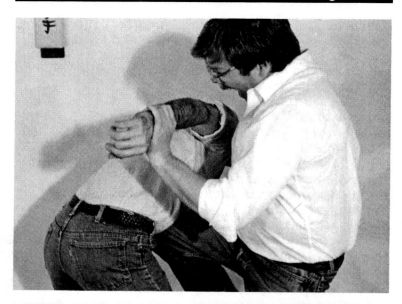

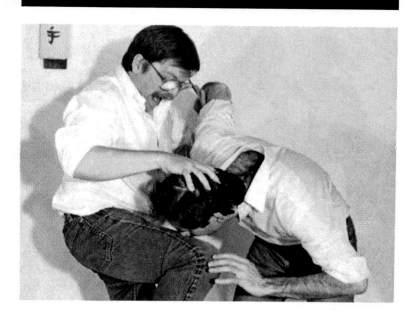

The defender forcefully drives the attacker's arm up as he pulls the head down (top left). This is done in one quick, snapping motion that doubles over the attacker to receive the rising knee strike to the midsection (ideally the solar plexus).

The knee to the midsection has further weakened and stunned the attacker. The impact has bounced the defender's hand off the attacker's neck (bottom left). The hand comes back down and lands on the back of the attacker's head, sometimes gripping the hair. Note how the defender has rotated his body from the previous photo while maintaining his grip at the attacker's wrist. This prevents the attacker from regaining any balance, making recovery impossible as long as he is kept in motion. This is similar in concept to "running the mark"; here we are spinning the mark. The defender uses this leverage to drive the attacker's face into the rising knee. This is a very strong, well-focused blow since the defender need only coordinate the impact of his own knee with his own hand.

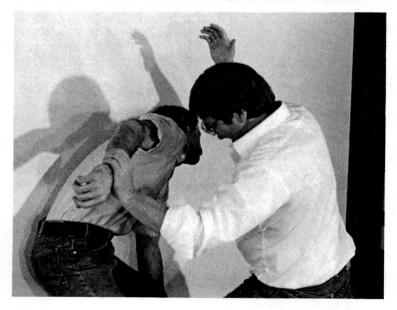

Once is not enough! The impact of the knee to the face has bounced the defender's hand up again; this time it comes down as a shuto to the neck. Note how the defender still maintains control and tactile feedback by retaining the attacker's right wrist. This entire sequence represents the concept of continuous attack.

THE VERTICAL FIST

In contrast to the position of the fist when a boxer throws a straight punch or hook, the vertical fist is held straight up and down. The wrist is bent slightly so that the line formed by the knuckles is essentially perpendicular to the floor and parallel to the vertical axis of the body.

The vertical fist is the first of the "acceleration-based" strikes we will examine. Acceleration-based blows move like a whip. They are fired into the target in one direction, then instantly reverse direction after contact is made. This is an essential concept you must understand to make these blows work. The drills will teach you how; here is the why.

Imagine a leather bullwhip and a watermelon. You cannot "stick" the flexible bullwhip into the watermelon. However, if you knew how to crack the whip (as you have seen in western movies), then you could blast a chunk out of the watermelon. To crack a bullwhip demands timing, and timing is the critical source of power in acceleration blows. If the whip arrives on target a little too early or too late, then there is no crack, thus no power. It is the same with the vertical fist. The candle drills will demonstrate this to you better than I can explain it.

For you physics freaks, here briefly are the mechanics of acceleration blows (you might as well skip this paragraph if you aren't into physics). Momentum is the simple product of mass x velocity. Keep in mind that acceleration is the second derivative of velocity and hence we have the equation: force = mass x acceleration. This simply gives us the "work" that will be done when something gives up its kinetic energy. Consider that acceleration can be positive or negative (deceleration). Near the point when the fist reverses, temporally and spatially we have a moment of extreme acceleration. Note that this is a brief interval only, and it occurs just before reversal. Also keep in mind that gravity and acceleration (or deceleration) are the same thing, quantum-wise.

This means the energy transfer is almost entirely a one-way street at that brief instant of collision. The guy's head takes the energy while the striking hand takes very little of the "rebound" energy. You can look at this several ways, but it all comes down to the extreme acceleration timed with the moment of impact and the reversal of the blow. This is what martial artists call "focus." There is real elegance to the simple mathematics of this situation. When done with near perfection, the power of such a

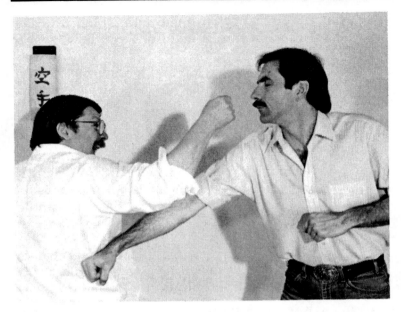

Vertical fist. The distance is somewhat exaggerated here to show the movement more clearly; things would be happening closer in a real fight. The defender has slipped the attacker's blow with the outside crane, and the vertical fist is being thrown from the outside gate. Note that the defender's eye is directly on the target. Impact will occur on the defender's first two knuckles. This blow is an acceleration-based blow; it whips out and back like a bullwhip.

blow becomes fantastic.

Remember I said you can't blast people in the head with a closed fist without risking injury to your hand? The vertical fist allows a blow to the head with a closed fist because of the whipping action and resulting energy transfer of the blow. In short, the power goes into his head rather than into your hand when the two collide. However, this one-way transfer of power demands proper focus of the blow.

The primary target for the vertical fist is the opponent's nose. The nose is an effective target (ever see a cat fight for its life against a big dog?) because, being soft tissue, it collapses under the blow and cushions the impact on your hand. The bony parts of the skull are too hard for this and the energy transfer is partly rebounded into your own hand. Like any strike, the vertical fist to the nose is not going to end the fight, but it will set up your next shot while your enemy is stunned and unable to effectively defend himself.

The second target for the vertical fist is the solar plexus. This is the area just below the sternum where the bottom ribs join in the front of your body. The solar plexus is an effective target for two reasons. Number one, this is where most of the heart is exposed. A focused blow here puts trauma on the heart, which can cause a momentary interruption in the pumping of blood. This interruption may only occur for a single heartbeat, but that's all you need to momentarily incapacitate your man. The second aspect of this shot, if it is powerful enough and your enemy isn't too large, is that it can force air out of the diaphragm, creating the classic "knocked out of wind" syndrome. (But keep in mind that no one blow is ever likely to be enough. People don't generally go down that easy.)

One of the advantages of the vertical fist is that it can be thrown effectively from a lot of odd angles. This is not the case with hooks, reverse punches, and so on because they demand the proper facing geometry position on your opponent to transmit power. The vertical fist does not demand such facing. The guy can be slightly behind and to the left of you, in front of you but so close his chest is right against yours, or a number of other odd angles where hooks and straight punches cannot be executed with maximum effect.

Another advantage is that the average dirtball is not familiar with this blow. One reason for this is that he does not see it often, so he has not learned to defend against it like he may have with other, more familiar blows like the straight punch or hook.

A third advantage, and this is real important, is that the vertical fist is much more difficult to see coming than a hook or even a straight punch. The hook has an arc to it, which gives the enemy a better chance to see it coming. The straight punch is harder to see because it takes a straight line in, but at eye level. The vertical fist is toughest of all because it begins its movement *below* the opponent's line of vision. The blow accelerates in the vertical plane, generally moving from waist level and rising into the nose or solar plexus. Because of the low path of the vertical fist, it can be thrown with power even when you are close to your opponent; too close, for example, for a reverse punch, hook, or straight punch to generate much power. It is also easier to uncork without telegraphing the blow.

The key to an effective vertical fist is holding the hand relaxed and partially open before the strike begins. As it rises into the target (with your eyes kept on the target), the hand is kept relaxed so it can move fast. Then it draws into a closed fist at impact. After impact, it instantly relaxes so it can return at once. The primary error in executing this blow is holding the hand and arm too tensely, thus providing resistance to the movement. This technique must have zip; it is a quick in/out shot. Your blow must be felt before it is seen (yeah, Bruce said this, too).

When you can regularly put out the candle with the vertical fist as outlined in the drills, you will have placed a formidable blow into your tool box of weapons.

Study the photos until you understand what is meant by all this. The vertical fist is one of only two closed-fist blows I use to an opponent's head. Here comes the next one.

THE BACKFIST

The backfist is also an acceleration blow. The striking area is the two large knuckles of your hand; the target is the opponent's temple or side of his lower jaw. Like the vertical fist, the hand is held open and loose on the way to the target so it can move unencumbered and quickly. Just before impact, the fist is pulled together and the hand locked out. After impact, the hand is again relaxed as it returns back to chamber as quickly as it went out.

The backfist, while thrown from the leading hand (the hand on the side of your body closest to your opponent), actually begins its acceleration from the hip furthest away from your opponent. Avoid swinging the blow out and away from your body any more than you need to generate power. It should travel close to your body. Martial arts instructors, especially traditionalists, have hard-and-fast rules for these blows. I have found that people's bodies differ, and this makes a difference as to how far the blow can swing out and away from the body before it loses power and is more easily blocked. Rather than be boxed in by a specific form, understand the following concepts and then experiment via the drills. Ultimately, you will find the correct path for the blow that fits your body.

The concepts to keep in mind are these. If the blow travels very close to your body, it makes it harder for the opponent to see before it lands. On the other hand, if the path of the blow is too close to your body, you restrain yourself by imparting tension on the arm, wrist, and hand. Letting the blow swing out a little will relax this tension and allow the fist to move faster and with greater effect. If the blow is thrown too far from the body, however, it loses power and becomes easier to intercept.

The backfist is another blow that the average guy is not familiar with. I almost always have used the backfist for an enemy in front of me or, less often, on an opponent who was hit but falling out of range. Since he was hurt, I could extend a little with a reaching backfist, possibly accompanied by a slight turn of my body to achieve a good angle.

The movies are big on showing the backfist used on an attacker grabbing or coming up from behind. In fact, the blow does not have much real juice when thrown at a guy behind you; it's just that it's one of the few shots you *can* execute from such a position. I can only remember one time when I used a backfist on an opponent who was behind me.

Now let's look at some drills for acceleration blows.

The Candle Drill

This drill provides you with feedback on the quality of your execution of the acceleration blow. You must keep trying until you get it right.

Get a round candle, about an inch in diameter, and light it. Using the vertical fist, attempt to put it out without actually touching it or the flame. This is accomplished by the compression of air that builds up in front of your hand just before the reversal of the blow. If you are focused correctly, it will be enough to blow out the candle. This demands some precision.

Most anybody, if they stay with it, can learn to put out the candle. Many people can learn to do it every other time after only an hour or so of practice. You should get this blow down to where you can do it just about every time.

When performing this drill, you will see how mental frustration at failure can make you try too hard. This means you are not relaxed. You can't power this exercise; in fact, the only way to put out the candle is with a properly focused blow.

Be sure to use a suitable candle. A candle that has a giant wick, a bevel, or too large a base that either shields the flame from the wind or does not let your hand get close enough before it hits the candle is no good. To get the idea and perhaps some encouragement that you can do it (always an important first step before actually doing anything), you can shave a bit of wax off the candle to make the flame more exposed.

Once you have it down, try putting out the candle from odd angles and while moving. An example is to stand just a little more than an arm's length away from the candle so you'll have to advance a little (slipping up with your feet) before uncorking the vertical fist. Many times in a fight, the execution of this blow demands and will be amplified by such an advance. In this way you learn to coordinate the two motions. (We will look at this in Chapter 5.)

For most (though not all) people, it is harder to perform the candle drill with the backfist, which is one reason to start off with the vertical fist. The physics of either blow is the same, however.

The Hanging Cloth Drill

Here we have another excellent training method. (An excellent training method is one that lets you know you are doing it right when the "trick" works and teaches you how at the same time.)

Take a piece of cloth, canvas, or old shower curtain. Cut the material into a square approximately eight by eight inches. Using string, suspend the material from the ceiling to about nose level.

The idea is to execute a vertical fist and later a backfist to make the cloth "pop." This occurs when the energy transfer is so quick that the cloth can't absorb it all without being displaced so rapidly that it "cracks" the air like the previously mentioned bullwhip. You will know when you do it right.

Experiment with all the mentioned materials and try different sizes. After you learn the basics, adjust the target height for taller and shorter victims. If you are really semipsycho, hang a number of targets around the house and, as you are walking by at odd times and angles, lash out with a sweetly focused vertical or backfist. My wife hates this.

THE PALM-HEEL STRIKE

The palm-heel strike is another favorite of mine that I have used many times to outstanding effect. Learn it and you can, too.

The splendor of the palm-heel strike is that it begins

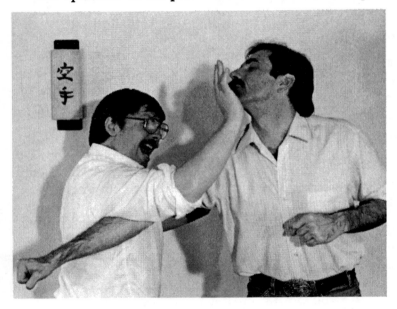

Palm-heel strike. In this photo, the blow is being thrown from the outside gate after the defender has executed an outside crane defense against a straight punch to his head. Note that in this gate position, the attacker's left hand is not available for an immediate blow; it has been drawn down by the outside crane (this hand action is shown in detail on pages 99-100). The defender's left hand is at the attacker's elbow, locking out the attacker's punching arm and continuing his forward motion into the palm-heel.

and ends with an open hand, and only the wrist locks out at the moment of impact. Thus it can move very fast, and this means power. Furthermore, the palm heel generates its force by imparting the strike with full body weight behind it. This is achieved by proper rotation of the hips (and it sometimes does not take much movement of the hips) and the timing of weight shift with the impact of the blow. You can hit most any target with this strike without much risk of injury to your hand.

The primary tactical advantage of the palm heel, however, is that it can be executed in a grappling or other close-in fighting situation. This generally means that the target for this blow is the solar plexus. It is also a good one to use to break the floating ribs if your opponent isn't too big (that is, if he doesn't have a much greater bone structure than you). A third target is a rising palm-heel under the opponent's chin, a more sophisticated form of the uppercut.

The palm-heel strike requires relaxation to generate speed, then "locking out" upon impact with the target. In this respect it shares elements with the two previous strikes. The essential contrast between the palm-heel strike and the vertical or backfist is that it is a *thrusting* blow more than an acceleration-based strike. While the acceleration blows are dependent on a reversal of the direction of the strike to convey power, the palm heel is generally thrown as a thrust *through* the body. Your arm and wrist should lock out as if they were one solid, nonarticulated weapon, like the end of a stick.

It is critical that the wrist be locked out on impact. This transmits the energy to the opponent's body rather than buckling your wrist. The striking surface is the bottom of the palm, which is in line with the junction of the ends of the ulna and radius bones and the carpus (just look at the photo).

Again, power comes from slightly rotating the hips so that as the blow arrives, your full body weight is riding with it. This demands a slight shift of weight; first to the rear leg, then to the forward leg. To get the proper hip action, experiment with holding your arm completely loose and snapping it up into the desired striking path by using your hips alone. You can't actually use the strike like this; this exercise is just to show you how a slight hip rotation facilitates power. You should also experiment with executing this strike as an acceleration blow.

THE REVERSE PUNCH

This is an acceleration-based strike that, like the palm-heel strike, uses hip rotation to shift body weight into the blow. Also like the palm-heel strike, it is useful almost exclusively against an opponent who is facing you squarely. It is often used in grappling situations.

The midsection is the only target for this blow, which again means the solar plexus and floating ribs. You will bust your hand if you use it to the head.

Taekwon-do people are big on the reverse punch and often execute it well in the dojang (the Korean equivalent of the Japanese dojo and Chinese kwoon). Unfortunately, most of them can't use it in a fight very well, but this is true of most karate techniques in most styles for most people. The karate sensei will tell you not to raise your rear heel when executing this blow. I have found that it is more practical to learn how to maintain balance while raising the rear heel to assist in transferring your weight into the blow.

Like all acceleration shots, the reverse punch must be retracted as quickly as it comes out. Again we see the familiar concept of relax on delivery, lock out on impact, then relax for the return. It is a whipping action.

Here are some drills for the palm-heel strike and reverse punch.

The Heavy Bag
Save your pennies, go down to a sporting goods store,

You must have something to hit with full power in order to develop a well-focused blow. This makes workouts on the heavy bag a necessity. Without such practice, your wrist is likely to buckle when striking an enemy. This can cause injury as well as absorb energy, which may make your blow ineffective. Use bag gloves to protect your hands. After you have trained a bit, experiment with lighter, unlined leather dress gloves. This will allow you to "feel" the impact on your hand better. In this way you train yourself to land the blow in such a manner as to reduce injury to your hand. This is essential, since you won't likely be wearing a glove in a real fight. On the other hand, if you do have a glove on in a real fight, it is a big advantage. Your heavy bag training will allow you to make the best of it.

and buy a heavy bag. The alternative is using a heavy bag at the local boxing academy or dojo, but having one in your own crib means you will practice more frequently and more freely. The heavy bag is also a good way to work off mental frustrations or a general piss-off in a way that won't get you into trouble.

While I list the heavy bag especially for the reverse punch and palm-heel strike, every blow should be practiced on it. There is simply no substitute for actually hitting something hard. Karateka punch at the air a lot, which often causes them real problems when it comes to a real battle. But learn the acceleration blows using the candle and cloth drills before taking on the heavy bag.

Yes you can bust your wrist or swell up your hands on the heavy bag if you don't do it right and don't *gradually* build up your power. You may discover your wrist buckles when hitting the bag. This must be eliminated. Without actually hitting something you would never realize that your wrist buckles up like this. You can't fix something until you know it's broke.

When working out on the heavy bag, use light bag gloves to protect your hands. Occasionally, try using dress gloves or unlined rawhide work gloves. You will notice how even a very light glove protects your hand much more than no glove at all. This is because the material tends to distribute the impact over a larger area of the hand. I mention this because when riding my scooter, I generally wear a rawhide glove to soak up vibration and protect my hands in case I have to lay the Serpent down. When I am forced to defend myself while I have that glove on (hasn't happened in a long time), then I will use some closed-fisted head shots that I would otherwise not employ with a bare hand. Knowing how to throw a strike, I can easily hit people harder than my hands can tolerate. But with rawhide gloves on, I can hit significantly harder with little risk to my hands. Experimenting on the bag with lighter gloves and sometimes a bare hand will show you how and where you have to be careful to avoid busting your hands on someone's skull.

When executing the reverse punch in particular, learn to throw a right/left/right combination to the same area in a continuous and rapid manner. You might get the chance for this combination in a real fight, and several well-focused blows to the same part of an opponent's body can have a cumulative effect.

With either the palm-heel strike or the reverse punch, your blow should penetrate *into* the bag. If the bag simply swings away on impact, then your focus isn't correct. A very powerful, well-focused blow will make the bag bend double before it starts moving back. This is because the focus is so well-timed, the power so great, and the energy transfer so quick that the bag does not have time to move back to absorb all that energy. Instead it bends before it moves. This is exactly what you want to happen to your opponent's body. To be more specific, you want his bones to bend before his body is moved back. You see, bones don't bend too well; they break.

THE SHUTO

The shuto is the knife hand or classic "karate chop" you have likely seen in movies or on television. It is a useful blow in real fights and I have used it frequently. Since it is an open-handed strike, it can be executed with speed, and it follows rather directly from your use of the open hand to slip your opponent's blow, as we will study in detail later.

The edge of the hand can strike a solid blow without busting the knuckles like a closed fist might. A shuto is more easily and naturally focused than a fist as well. It places a lot of force on a relatively small area of the opponent's anatomy when it connects. The best targets are the side of the neck and the clavicle.

When executed properly against the side of the neck,

the shuto can be a very stunning blow. It can also break the clavicle of most people, assuming the person being hit and the guy doing the hitting have about the same size bone structure. Unfortunately, in the dynamic action of a real fight, it takes skill and experience to connect properly with this blow and break a guy's clavicle. On the other hand, if you do bust the clavicle, which is about the easiest bone to break in the whole body, the fight is over.

Previously, I said to not count on any single blow to end a fight, and this is still true. So don't count on the shuto to the clavicle to end the fight. It's not that easy a shot to deliver properly to such a specific target, especially when your opponent is moving real quick and punching at your head. But if you do break his clavicle, he will no longer be able to fight with any effectiveness since he will not be able to use either of his arms. You see, the clavicle on one side of the body holds down the fulcrum for the arm on the other side. He might try to swing, but it won't work; the mechanical linkage just isn't there anymore, and his effort will cause him enormous pain.

If you break your opponent's clavicle, then step back and let the guy go, but do not drop your defense. You don't need to pound him anymore because he can't hurt you anymore. Just be certain that you have broken the bone cleanly before breaking off your attack. (I've broken a few people's clavicles; you can feel it break just like a stack of pine boards.)

Like all the other strikes, your arm must be relaxed to execute a good shuto strike. It can be used as either an acceleration or power blow—the former snaps back and the latter cracks down with your body weight behind it. The acceleration version is the better way to go, especially to the neck. But when you have hurt your man enough to slow things down a bit, then the power version can be a good knockout shot or bone breaker.

The shuto will knock people out for an instant if you hit them behind the neck with enough force, and it does not take much force. We have all seen this in the fantasyland of movies and television. My only problem with the way they do it is in getting my opponent to turn around so I can hit him there. Generally, he just won't want to cooperate like that. Occasionally during grappling you can get this behind-the-neck shot if the guy is holding on to you and puts his head down to drive you into something or knock you off your feet. Most of the time, however, you will have to settle for a shuto to the side of his neck.

It is worthwhile to learn how to throw alternating shutos using just one hand to the left and right sides of your enemy's neck. They have a peculiarly cumulative effect—the one nerve group is shocked just as the other is "recovering." I have used this on guys who've managed to get me down on the floor and were on top of me (I hate it when that happens). Practice this move on your back with your partner on top of you.

I learned this little trick from a taekwon-do gentleman who was fresh off a flight from Seoul to officiate at a testing and promotion session. This man was a fourth dan (fourth-degree black belt), and I have no doubt that it is not too much to say that taekwon-do was his life. I was teaching another style and arranged a friendly athletic contest with this man, a very pleasant and courteous individual. One doesn't get many chances to free spar with a fourth dan who has trained exclusively in the Orient. I was looking to test some advanced techniques I'd been working on and was really hoping to learn something from him. In fact I did learn something from this guy . . . just before he almost knocked me out.

Now that it comes back to me, there are a couple of lessons in this tale about tactics and techniques that should be useful to you, particularly if you study or plan to study some martial art form. Let me give you some background.

One of the heavily emphasized concepts in taekwon-do is perfect facing and the geometry of power in linear strikes. In contrast, I had always favored the circular patterns. My feeling was that the rigid, robot stances and movements of taekwon-do were simply not fast, fluid, and transitionally smooth enough for effective real fighting. Indeed, I'd experienced a number of taekwon-do black belts go soft and circular on me when I pressed them hard in free sparing.

On the other hand, I also realized that if taekwon-do shots connected like they were meant to, then they were real bone shatterers. Yet all that perfectly straight shoulders and precise stances for the delivery or blocking of a blow did not seem real appropriate to me if your opponent isn't fighting that way, too. Of course, taekwon-do people generally only spar with taekwon-do people, so this doesn't often come up as a problem for them, except maybe when they get into real fights. Still, if the taekwon-do stylist is fast enough and has proper fighting spirit and good power, he can certainly make the taekwon-do approach work in an actual fight.

Taekwon-do is also real big on kicking and even kick combinations rather than on hand techniques. In real fights, I found kicks to be dangerous to try or just not very effective, while good hand techniques were indispensable.

It may sound arrogant, but taekwon-do people (except for a few who didn't fight like taekwon-do people) had never given me much problem in these athletic contests. They all seemed to fight the same way and could be set up and feinted the same way. The chance to fight a forth dan from Korea would perhaps give me a chance to see a person dedicated to his art and talented enough to make all that stuff work.

I had been studying a Chinese system under a

Vietnamese guy, Anh Van Nyuen, for about a year. I'd previously studied a number of arts to beyond intermediate levels.

On top of this, I had been working on a very advanced and somewhat esoteric technique of blocking a series of reverse punches to the midsection. I knew this technique wasn't going to be of much, if any, value in real fights, but that wasn't the point. I just wanted to see if my theory could be mechanically made to work in the laboratory of the dojo. In brief, this technique used the power of an opponent's blow to reverberate your hand in a series of rebounding arcs such that each of his reverse punches knocked your hand into his other wrist and back again between his two punches. In effect, he blocked his own shots at his own rhythm.

Curiously, to make it work, the guy throwing the reverse punches would have to do them almost perfectly and in the classic manner. (You can see why this wasn't a practical fighting technique since most people don't attack like that in real fights.) But I figured if anybody might, it would be this ranking taekwon-do man. This would give me a chance to try out my move.

Before the match, the guy wore me out somewhat by making me execute a bunch of techniques (taekwon-do techniques, naturally) before he would allow me the honor of the contest. Not being oriented to his style, I thought my stuff was a little sloppy (maybe more than a little sloppy), but he accepted me for a light-contact, full-speed match.

The Korean opened the match with the customary bow of his form. I returned this bow and then executed the Chinese white crane kung-fu salute just to try to shake him up psychologically. I guess he'd never seen this form of salute before because it did seem to put a curious look on his face.

I attacked at once and with power. I was able to drive him back for a moment, but he deftly blocked all my shots in a very classic fashion. So far he was making the straight Korean forms work pretty good.

Then he uncorked a roundhouse kick to my head that I still don't see how he managed to get off. It was blocked, but it carried a lot of power, and that slowed down my blocking hand for the counterattack. Incredibly, without any hesitation or telegraphing, he actually went into a spinning heel kick with the same leg! This was full-on movie shit now. I never thought anybody could chain kicks that fluidly. He still wasn't hitting me with them, but his kicks gave me no chance to counterattack. He uncorked a series of at least four or five kicks that drove me back. All I could do was block them one after another. He jumped up for a flying side kick and, once he landed, executed another spin kick! I had never seen anything like it except in the movies. He was driving me across the mat in a straight line so quickly with these impossible techniques that I could not sidestep or move to the corner as I'd always been able to do before.

The next thing I knew my feet were on the bare floor. I had been driven off the mat and my back was against the wall. The Korean's body came down squarely in front of me very close and with perfect facing as he executed his first offensive hand techniques of the match, a series of perfectly focused reverse punches to my midsection.

I was perceptually ready for these blows, yet there was absolutely no way I could avoid them except by means of that esoteric technique I'd been practicing. While he didn't exactly telegraph his punches, he may have slowed down a fraction of a second since he certainly thought he had me and could afford to take the extra time to perfectly square off the blows. This helped, because I knew instinctively that these were the shots that had to come next.

When I looked down at his fists, I saw my own hand bouncing between them, blocking them perfectly through the use of his own power. Nobody was more amazed than myself. Since his blows drove the defense, my blocks had his timing and rhythm. It was very much like a musician's drumstick reverberating on a drumhead, only the drumstick was my hand and it was reverberating between his two wrists.

For a split second the beauty of this technique stopped my mind, but at once I realized the Korean was also transfixed so I did not hesitate. I executed a backfist to his head with full *kiai!* The blow was clearly good—well focused and plenty of juice. His hands were still at midgate so he was unable to block. I stopped it a fraction from actually striking the man, then immediately threw him with *usoto gari* (a judo leg throw). When he hit the ground, I came down on him to execute an overhead hammer fist to his nose.

There were at least a hundred people watching this match, and I had a fourth dan from Korea on his back and in a split second I was going to finish him off decisively for everybody to see. In the passion of the moment, Musashi's warning had been forgotten. I was thinking of victory and myself.

As I moved down on him, the Korean reached up and pulled me into him. Gravity had been my ally, but he instantly reversed this situation by pulling me in the same direction I was going. Instinctively, I had to catch myself from falling into him. At that instant he pulled me into a series of alternating shutos on either side of my neck using his right hand.

His blows were very well-controlled, and he wasn't trying to hurt me. But I'm sure he could have. While he didn't hit me very hard, the shutos were perfectly focused and hit my neck absolutely perpendicularly. I believe he hit me four times, twice on each side of the neck.

The effect of his blows was quite remarkable. My vision grayed, and I was essentially "out on my feet" for a moment. After a second or so (maybe less) of incapacitation, I stood up, bowed to acknowledge his victory, and that was that.

Through an interpreter (as I speak almost no Korean and his English was on the same level), we had a good talk afterward.

While my esoteric blocking technique had proved itself, I hardly gave it anymore thought or practice. I knew I'd never get a chance to use it in a real fight for precisely the reasons it had worked on the Korean. On the other hand, I now had a useful new tool. I would have previously considered his simple alternate shutos to be a "slight technique." (A slight technique is one that could perhaps be executed in a real fight but is unlikely to have the power to incapacitate.) This match showed me that this was not a slight technique at all. On the contrary, I began to practice the Korean's technique because he had shown me its practical value.

Nevertheless, my basic reservations about taekwon-do went unchanged. Just because a talented and dedicated master might be able to make something work does not mean it is the best way to go, or even that the technique is of any value to most people. After all, few of us have that much dedication, fewer still the talent, and almost none of us will ever become masters. I certainly include my beer-swilling, scooter-trash self here.

Okay, we were looking at the basic blows. The next one is simple enough—that hammer fist that I had hoped to execute on the Korean.

THE HAMMER FIST

The hammer fist is a power blow. It uses full body weight to achieve its force. It is not an acceleration-type strike in any way. It is not used much by sucker punchers, streetfighters, or karateka for that matter because it is a pretty easy blow to see coming and therefore fairly easy to block or at least partially block.

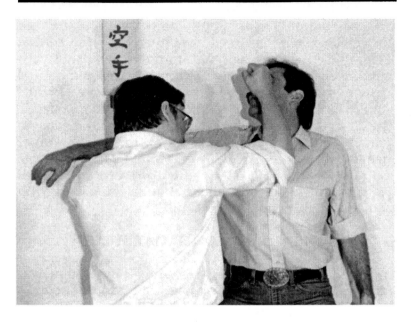

The hammer fist. This is a very powerful blow that you can strike to the head without hurting your hand. However, it is only used against an injured or stunned opponent, since otherwise it is rather easily blocked. Here, the opponent has been spun into the wall with a wrist/throat spinout. The hammer fist is landed as he hits the wall, which makes the blow more effective since, being trapped against the wall, his body cannot be forced backward by the blow. This means he absorbs all the energy of the strike with his head.

This is why the hammer fist is reserved for use on an opponent who is already stunned or otherwise hurt such that his defenses are not fully operational. Examples include after you have just cracked your man with a solid elbow to the head, knee to the solar plexus, alternate shutos to the neck, and so on. It can sometimes be used the instant after you run your opponent's body into the wall, post, floor, etc.

The hammer fist is simply the bottom of the closed fist crashing into the target, most often after a somewhat looping overhead arc to build up power. You shift your entire weight into the blow at impact. This is a natural blow that is not hard to learn. But do you see why it's easy to block or dodge if used on a fully alert opponent?

This strike is used to transmit maximum power to your target when speed and deception are no longer needed to make it land. Targets are the nose or the clavicle. By striking with the bottom of the fist, you protect your hand from injury should you collide with something real solid, like his skull.

OPEN-HANDED THROAT SHOT

This blow has but a single target—the opponent's throat. The striking area on your hand is the area between your thumb and index finger. This strike is thrown very similarly to the palm-heel strike in terms of relaxation, then lock-out.

This blow has many names in different martial arts systems, but knowing the Asian name of a technique isn't going to help you in a real fight. I just call it the open-handed throat shot. I have used this blow many times and have found that very few people can take it *if* you can connect. Again, this is a blow that is struck with the open hand, which makes it a natural counterstrike after slipping your opponent's blow with the open hand.

This technique can be executed either as an acceleration or thrust strike. I prefer to use it as an acceleration blow that snaps out and back real fast. The throat is pretty soft tissue and won't put much stress on the striking hand. It is also a very sensitive part of the anatomy since blows to this area can really screw up a guy's breathing. When landed, it can stun a person so well that he won't be able to see or coordinate defensive moves for an instant, allowing you to follow up at once with a power blow like the hammer fist or palm-heel strike.

Ideally, this strike begins at your hip and accelerates all the way to the target. As before, you are not simply striking with your hand—your hips are in the blow as well. This is true regardless of whether you use it as a thrust or acceleration strike. No blow works unless it can land on target, and you get this blow on target by not letting your enemy see it coming. This is accomplished by throwing the blow from a rising arc that begins below his field of vision and suddenly is inside his field of vision. A blow that accelerates in a vertical plane close to the opponent's body often remains unseen until he's struck. This deceptive aspect makes this blow similar to the vertical fist.

Drills for the Hammer Fist and
Open-Handed Throat Shot

The hammer fist is a natural for the heavy bag. Note how much force you can use by striking the bag this way and still not cause a lot of pain in your hand. Start out slow and get the form such that you shift your weight into the blow and land squarely with the bottom of your fist. Place small pieces of tape on the bag at various heights to represent the opponent's nose or clavicle.

Your hammer fist should not swing out too much in the horizontal plain. This blow begins at your hip and follows an overhead arc into the bag. There is a slight whip out of the vertical plane for power, but otherwise do not allow the blow to swing out too far. Again, this results in less power and makes it easier for your opponent to see and block. Find the right path for your body that balances these two considerations.

The open-handed throat shot presents more of a training problem because the blow wraps into the throat, which is shaped like a cylinder and is soft. Thus you can't realistically execute it on the heavy bag. The candle drill is

Open-handed throat shot. Here we see a realistic depiction of this blow in terms of distance. This blow is being thrown from the inside gate after the defender has executed an inside crane defense. Notice that the defender has advanced on the attacker with his right leg as he strikes with his right hand to the throat. This is an example of the sliding-up advance and strong-side-forward facing. The defender has slipped his forward leg between and behind the attacker's legs, which makes him safe while the attacker is virtually helpless.

useful, but the technique tends to become a palm-heel shot since the striking area for the throat shot is the webbed area between thumb and index finger. It's kind of tough to put the candle out with this area of the hand since the thumb and fingers arrive before the striking area.

I have tried a number of training methods for this shot but have yet to find the ideal one. At one point, I bought a bunch of three-quarter-inch wooden dowels at the hardware store and snapped them in two with a quick in/out acceleration-based strike. It was almost too easy, though curiously hard on the hand. The rawhide glove helped and also eliminated the occasional splinter problem. Breaking wooden dowels was of value, but it was a bit of a chore to set them up in a vertical plane so that they would be supported rigidly enough to break.

Another method I used was to fill a bicycle tube full of sand and hang it, like a miniature version of the heavy bag. The blow was executed correctly when the tube buckled before it moved back. The tube will expand to represent various neck sizes, but the sand gets pretty heavy if you make the diameter too large. Another problem was the sand was still pretty rough on the hands. Try mixing it with pearlite (small Styrofoam balls used to lighten the soil mixture for potted plants). It is cheap; you find it in the houseplant section of the supermarket. Don't use too much or the target will be too light. The tube must be heavy enough to offer realistic resistance to the blow. This method can also be used to develop your vertical fist as well.

ELBOW AND KNEE STRIKES

These are your close-in fighting weapons. Close-in fighting techniques, including the grappling aspect of fighting, are often the ones that decide the outcome of a fight. Personally, I prefer fighting my opponent right up next to him, with my chest nearly touching his. I have discovered that it is often safer to be inside your man than at the limits of his reach. Also, most people try to move away when I close on them this way, which means I'm controlling them and forcing them into a "reactive" fight.

There are three basic distances in a fight. First is long range; this is leg or kicking distance. Next is hand distance. Finally, there's knee and elbow distance. In most real fights you won't have much choice; your opponent will generally force you into a given distance, at least initially. (I am, of course, assuming you are not the aggressor.)

Elbows and knees are larger than hands and can take a lot of shock before they are damaged. In fact, you can strike to the hard bones of a person's skull with a knee and often an elbow without busting your striking limb. Of course, the trick is to get his head down there so you can use your knee.

The three targets for the knee are the groin, midsection, and face. All demand that you control your opponent's body to make these targets accessible. The wrist and neck spinout is useful in getting your opponent doubled over for head and face strikes with the knee.

The most useful elbow strikes are the horizontal elbow and front forearm strike. They are best directed to the opponent's throat. A secondary target is the solar plexus. The rear elbow's target is the side of the head; it is powerful against an opponent at your rear and very close (holding onto you), but the fact is I have had very few chances to use it in real fights (the front forearm and front elbow strikes are quite another matter). This strike is real good when somebody is trying to choke you from the front with both hands on your throat. This is a stupid way to choke somebody, but I've seen it go down plenty of times. If someone chokes you like this and you know the elbow strike and don't panic, they are in for the purple lights against the black background as your blow rattles their brain.

In delivering these strikes, relaxation is the key. Lock them out as they arrive, not before. The rear elbow strike is best delivered as a full body weight blow, with proper hip torque. The front elbow strike can be executed as either an acceleration blow or a thrusting shot. If you are real large boned, go for the thrust version. If you are smaller boned or if you are especially limber and fast, go for the snappy acceleration approach.

While the elbow and knee can deliver a lot of power with less chance of injury than the smaller mass of the hands or feet, you can still bust your elbow or kneecap. I busted my elbow on a guy. It took a long time to heal, too. Avoid such injury by training on the heavy bag and striking with the forearm rather than the point of the elbow. This is a less-focused blow, but it is safer and still has plenty of juice.

Once again, by actually hitting the heavy bag with full power, you can discover both how to deliver a more powerful blow and how to decrease the odds of injuring the striking area. Pain helps you out this way by telling you if your focus is off and energy is transferring back into your hand, or if you are focusing too much power on the point of the elbow, and so forth.

The heavy bag is ideal training for these blows, but imagine a guy who is so fast and snappy and has such control that he can put out the candle with his elbow or knee strikes! I once saw a muay-thai fighter (Thai kickboxer) doing just that. These fighters are generally smaller, lighter-boned men. Their training is ungodly tough and basically full contact all the time. Luckily, you most likely won't have to fight anybody with this kind of skill, determination, or technique.

One of the techniques used by these muay-thai fighters (and, curiously, by Enshin karate men) is the shin kick to the ribs or face. Experiment with this blow on the heavy bag to see if it can work for your body type. It's like a roundhouse kick that lands with the shin rather than the foot.

THE IMPORTANCE OF HAVING
WELL-FOCUSED SHOTS IN YOUR TOOL BOX

I had a very close friend of more than twenty years, Quick Carl, also known as "The Kaliem." He is now deceased. May he dine on Golden Lamb in Paradise! Our adventures were many. There is a certain bond that develops between comrades who have faced their death together. The Kaliem and I felt the devil fighting for our ass more than once.

In later life we tended to get a little out of hand on occasion, especially when we got together for a good time. I guess this behavior was sort of subconsciously our way of saying to ourselves, "I'm still here! I'm still here!" We were alive, and to watch us party you damn well knew it.

The Kaliem was a black man. As matter of fact, he was very black. One of his favorite pastimes was "chasing the white gals." This caused us some problems here and there. On one particular occasion it almost got us dusted. Hence the point of my story about the value of having a well-focused blow.

We had been partying pretty heavy at a hotel bar/disco. (Remember disco? The fact that it's now gone serves as some proof that there may be a God after all.) Since this was a pretty high-class place, combined with the fact that I was on my ninth or tenth bourbon, I guess I wasn't as *aware* as I should have been.

Apparently, three cowboy types objected to our presence and behavior. I failed to notice same and they ambushed us as we left the establishment. There was some new construction going on which forced us down a makeshift plywood hallway to get to the parking lot. Carl had the point. My mind was a light-year away from any thought of a physical hassle. I should have known better. If I had been aware, I could have avoided the whole setup.

When Carl went through the hallway's exit, he took a couple of steps before being blindsided by one of these guys with some sort of stick. Carl was knocked out instantly and later hospitalized for a concussion and hairline skull fracture. If I had been in the lead, I would have likely gone down the same way.

I must have switched instantly to combat mode because I was on the guy and disarmed him of his stick before I really knew where I was or what was going on. But there were three guys and one tackled me to the ground. I lost both the stick and my glasses. I can't see too good without my glasses, especially at night.

The guy was on top of me grappling with me on the ground while the others were kicking me from the sides. Instinctively, I reached down the front of the guy's jeans and grabbed his balls. I heard myself scream as I yanked them with all my power and then delivered a head butt that even made me see little points of purple light against a black background.

The next thing I knew I was standing up and the other two guys were punching me all over. My head was in a fog. I must have been blocking or breaking the focus of their blows, but I really can't say I was aware of such action. What I do remember is sort of going Frankenstein on them. You know; when the monster moves kind of slow but nothing seems to stop him.

I clearly recall holding on to each individual I needed to hit and basically ignoring the other guy, even though he was punching me. While holding the guy with my left, I gave a *kiai* (just like in the old dojo) as I executed well-focused reverse punches to his ribs. I had no way out and my adrenaline was pumped up to the max. The result was that my blows shattered his ribs each time they landed. In contrast, though these guys were pounding the hell out of me, their blows were simply not doing the damage mine were.

At the time I was not truly aware of the particular strikes I was using. In retrospect, I believe I only used the reverse punch, shuto, and hammer fist. (This conclusion was drawn from the medical reports on the guys after they were discovered and taken to the local emergency room.)

The two standing guys had multiple broken ribs. One of them had a collapsed lung from a fractured rib splintering into it. The other had broken floating ribs and a fractured clavicle. The guy I grappled with on the ground was hospitalized but had no broken bones as I recall.

I broke a toe, most likely from kicking the bastards after they were on the pavement. I also broke a bone in my right hand, the only hand I used to strike blows in the fight. Other than that and multiple bruises on my abdomen, skinned knees, and a cut on my forehead, I was okay.

The thing that kept me from getting beaten to a pulp by these guys (who I think would have done a lot worse to us if things had gone as they planned) was my ability to strike a well-focused blow capable of breaking bones. They hit me more times than I hit them—my blows were just more effective. The heavy bag will train you to deliver such a blow.

However, this is the real world, people. If you are very small and your opponent very large, it may be impractical for you to pursue a bone-breaking strategy. Still, you must train to deliver the maximum-power blow that your body and mind are capable of delivering. Keep in mind that most fights are not "no way out" situations such as I described here. In general, you won't have to knock your assailant out. Most of the time you just need to prevent him from hitting you. This can sometimes be accomplished by slipping his initial shot and instantly returning a counterstrike that stuns him enough for you to escape.

This particular fight was one of those rare instances where there was no way out. I had to fight these guys until either they or I were down for the count. Otherwise, both me and my buddy would have been stomped until we sustained permanent and disabling injuries at the least. As it was, my friend needed surgery from the stick blow.

There is more to this little tale.

I took my friend to the hospital and left that trash bleeding in the parking lot. About a month later I was arrested for a number of major crimes of violence over this incident and had to post $10,000 in bail. For several months I faced a trial and possible prison sentence. The judge would not even grant me bail at first because of "the particularly vicious nature of the assault and the seriousness of the injuries of the victims." This is not the twilight zone, people; this is exactly what happened.

I was unaware that anybody saw the fight, but lucky for me some people did. Also lucky for me, I had worked briefly for a detective agency in this town where I'd lived for some years. Nothing too glamorous—mainly process serving and skip tracing. I did not know my employer very well, but he really came through for me. Old "Max" found those people who saw the fight, and they gave depositions to the DA. Max also got the rap sheets on this vermin. Every one of the guys who jumped us had prior major felony convictions.

In the end, I was never even indicted on the charges. But all the legal shit took almost three months and it caused my wife and me a lot of anxiety.

The moral: stay out of fights if at all possible. If you have no way out, then be sure you have a well-focused blow. Train on the heavy bag.

SOME CONCLUSIONS ABOUT THE VARIOUS STRIKES AND TRAINING METHODS

I have only covered a handful of blows in this chapter. There are dozens more, and I haven't even listed any kicks at all. While we will eventually look at a few more strikes, the ones I have described here are the ones I used almost exclusively while working in the bar and occasionally in street battles. You do not need a lot of techniques in real fights! (Say, have I already said that?)

Now, about training. If you just read this book and don't engage in any of the training drills, you are just fooling yourself if you think you have increased your self-defense ability. Go out and get that heavy bag, hang it up, and use it! Do the drills with the cloth, candle, and sand-filled inner tube. Go real slow with no real impact at first to achieve correct form and feel the correct impacting surface on your body.

A little training really can help a great deal to increase the power of your strikes. If the first time you hit something solid is in your first real fight, buddy, that is likely going to be too late. Work so you can put out that candle with a crisp vertical fist and make that heavy bag double up with an elbow strike. It feels good when you know the blow is executed right and with power. This confidence may help you as much as the technique itself in a real fight.

Keep these fundamentals in mind. Power comes from the correct use of *speed, acceleration, and body weight*. The central inhibitor of speed is mental tension that results in tense muscles before the strike. The drills (the candle drill in particular) will teach you focus and acceleration. You must perform them.

I call this chapter the toolbox because that's all you have when you learn how to throw a good blow—a tool. Using the tool effectively is an entirely different matter. To a significant extent, you can learn to simply execute the blow with the drills and equipment I mentioned here. But delivering the blow effectively in a fight is quite different.

Furthermore, to learn the dynamics of defense (that is, avoiding the opponent's blow), you must have training partners. Without a good practical knowledge of avoiding an opponent's blow, you may never get a chance to use any strikes; you will probably be put out of the picture before you are able to fight. It's like a baseball player with a monster swing—if he can't connect with the ball, he's out. His swinging power becomes irrelevant. In a real fight, you won't get three swings before you are out. Generally, you only get that first one, hence the importance of avoiding the full power of the enemy's opening shot.

Finally, keep in mind the components of speed. Relaxation is the key to speed in every way. But how relaxed are you going to be when someone is seriously blasting away at you with lefts and rights to your head? This is a real problem for most everyone. There is no way I can explain in a book how to remain relaxed during a fight. This does, however, identify one of your goals. It will be one of the most important measures of your progress in developing your ability to make things work in a fight.

Consider the counter example. A guy has trained in karate to some degree, but with very little contact. A sucker puncher hits him in the head. The guy has never been really hit in the head before. He instinctively covers up and puts his head down to protect it. Now he can't see anything. He hasn't got any visual cues and no tactile feedback on his attacker's movements. The result? The guy gets blasted one shot after another, each blow leaving him less able to defend himself. This is really the typical situation. In fact, the sucker puncher counts on it going this way.

Do you see that the "instinctual" reaction—putting the head down and all that—was not the best response here? Indeed, it left the guy unable to defend himself at all. He had never been hit real hard in the head before, so his lack of experience gave him little chance to deal with it instantly and effectively. He could only pull in, both physically and mentally. The guy became his own worst enemy because he could not relax enough to control his own mind and body. He could not make use of any attack or defense techniques he'd ever learned.

Now consider an alternative situation. The guy being attacked is a student of Western boxing. When he takes the sucker punch, he sees stars, too. But he has been hit before, since all his training is basically full contact. The result, even though he may be dazed, is that he grapples with his attacker. The boxer ties up the guy's arms, preventing him from delivering another good, focused shot, which is just what he does in the practice ring when he's in trouble.

Now, in the next second or two, since the boxer is not taking full-force head shots anymore, he starts to move. He *sees* his attacker by feeling the body shifts while they clinch. Now the sucker puncher breaks away in order to get the distance and leverage for another head shot. But what happens? The sucker puncher hasn't protected himself in the break and catches a good left hook from the boxer on the way out, followed by a quick, powerful right. Now maybe the sucker puncher is hurt and grappling to tie up some arms.

What is the difference between these two scenarios, both of which I have seen played out more than a few times?

The first and obvious difference is in training methods. Contact versus no contact. But the training method made the difference principally in the manner in which the two individuals responded after being hit. One guy had developed no other abilities but to pull in both physically and mentally. The other guy's body operated on autopilot. In protecting himself with the clinch, he gave himself the chance to respond the instant his head cleared. He was able to use previous training effectively in a new situation, a real fight. To sum it up, the different training methods made the difference because they developed different *attitudes* on the part of the defenders.

Techniques are in the toolbox once you put them there through training. But if you can't develop the proper combat attitude, *your toolbox remains locked!*

CHAPTER 4

PRINCIPLES OF DEFENSE

The primary objective of defense is to avoid being hit. However, a very important secondary goal of an effective defense strategy is to place yourself in a strong position for a counterattack once you have avoided your opponent's blow.

Keep in mind, the subject of this book is applied self-defense in the real world. We are not interested in "scoring points" on our attacker. Any counterstrike must stun your opponent enough to, a) allow you to safely escape, or b) set up an opening for several continuous follow-up strikes to disable him. The first goal is a lot easier than the second.

Moreover, it is generally not necessary to drop your opponent to the ground unconscious. This can take time, and the longer the fight lasts the more likely you are to get hurt. You want to get it over with as quickly as possible. Escaping works real good in this regard, but so will knocking your man unconscious if the circumstances require it.

Let me give you an example of an "escape" scenario.

The sucker puncher, generally after (but maybe during) one of the aforementioned "interview" sessions, throws a blindside overhead right to your head. Because you have read this book and did the drills with a training partner, you are able to avoid the full force of the shot. The blow skins across your face; you are a little stunned, but your response is still immediate and continuous.

Without blocking his blow or contesting his power, and without arresting his forward motion, you have still managed not to be blasted out of the picture with his opening shot. Your open hand that slipped his blow now returns into his throat with an open-handed throat strike. The sucker puncher not only takes the force of your blow, but the impact is compounded by his own forward motion. He is significantly, though perhaps only momentarily, disabled. You are still in motion and, again, with the same hand, you throw a shuto to the side of his neck as you step past him in a run for the door. Remembering Chapter 1, however, you yell out for everyone to hear while running for the exit, "Get away from me! Leave me alone!" There is no mention of "You asshole" or "I'll kill you!" in your little declaration to the crowd.

Now, there are several possible outcomes. One is that the bouncer, having been alerted by your actions and seeing you running for the door, instinctively and immediately looks for someone chasing you and, in particular, if they have a weapon. Your attacker, usually twice your size, has recovered enough to begin chasing you. His intent is to pound your face into raspberry jam.

But the bouncer is experienced in his craft. Without alerting your pursuer to his presence before contact, the bouncer applies necessary and lawful force to restrain him. This may come in the form of a clothesline shot to the throat, sending the bastard down hard to the barroom floor, or any of a number of moves he has used before. You, after all, have made it easy for the bouncer. He likes this. You tried to avoid trouble. On the other hand, the bouncer may be very cross with your attacker because that guy's a troublemaker.

In fact, if you are lucky, the bouncer has had to deal with this guy before and has been waiting for a chance to put his lights out and eighty-six the slime from the establishment forever. Oh, the happy day!

The bouncer isn't too worried about legal problems at this point. After all, everybody heard you scream out and try to get away. It was unmistakable who the aggressor was and who had to be "restrained." He was just doing his duty. Of course he's sorry the guy ended up with those broken bones but hell, he had to defend himself and that guy was pretty big!

If you want things to work out like this, study this book, do the drills with a training partner, and avoid trouble in the first place.

You might say, "Yeah, but what if no bouncer magically appears to save me while I'm on my way to the door?" Good question; glad you asked. In this case, you have extended to yourself the same legal protection "after the fact" that you provided the bouncer in the previous scenario.

Again, you must have a clear and relaxed mind while fleeing from the guy. Can you make it to the door and into your car, to the other side of the bar, or some other safe place? Maybe not. In that case, realize that there are few people easier to ambush than somebody who is chasing you and is boiling mad to get you. All you need is a little time, a little distance between you and him, and some previous study of the problem.

A Vietnamese friend of mine, and a good martial artist, was being chased like this once. The guy chasing him literally was twice his weight. My buddy, despite his martial skill, was no fool and did not try to square off with this guy. Instead he ran about halfway up some stairs, allowing the guy to get just close enough before he whirled around and kicked him in the face.

The shot was real poetry. Since Anh was higher up than his victim, the kick had real power because it did not have to rise much above the waist. It dropped the guy down the stairs, but my pal didn't lose an instant as he continued up the stairs to the street and disappeared.

You can learn to spin around and ambush a guy who is chasing you if you give it some practice beforehand. I can tell you from experience that this is a useful skill in real fighting. But contrast this with training in a martial arts school. They won't even get into the idea of escaping, much less reversing in flight for the ambush.

I will paraphrase Musashi: "Some people practice their swordsmanship only in the training hall. But, you will not always meet your enemy in the training hall. You must practice in the rice paddy, on uneven ground, and in the tea room." Like most of the grim swordsman's advice, there is more to this little pearl of wisdom than its obvious meaning.

Seems like an appropriate place for another quote from Musashi's *A Book of Five Rings:* ". . . if you learn 'indoor' techniques, you will think narrowly and forget the True Way. Thus you will have difficulty in actual encounters."

Now, for you guys who have studied some martial arts, this "being pursued" scenario is one of the few practical uses for the back kick or rear thrust kick. However, your timing has to be very good. Pad up your training partner and make contact as you are running off the mat and he is chasing you. Then practice on stairs, in the hallway, on wet grass, or anywhere.

The palm heel to the solar plexus or under the chin or the open-handed throat shot are easier to pull off after spinning around. First turn your head to see your target before the rest of your body completes the spin. This is faster than spinning wildly, which is ineffectual if you don't connect on target. Also, use the turn as a hip rotation to amplify the blow.

I'm not going to get into these "turning on the pursuer" attacks too much. You must discover the problems of this situation by working with a partner. The primary point is that it is a valuable skill for escaping from a pursuing attacker in a real fight. If you practice it, even for a modest amount of time, you will discover and thus eliminate the basic mistakes you would otherwise make. However, if you have to try it for the first time when you are actually being chased by a beserko, then you won't have a real good chance of pulling it off.

Before I leave this topic, note what Mako said after he clubbed his attacker into unconsciousness with a telephone receiver: "The warrior uses what is at hand. There is no shame in this." When being pursued in your escape flight, be alert for such improvised weaponry as a pool cue, beer bottle, or even a beer tray. Whipping a chair into a guy's head has worked pretty good for me on occasion. Interposing another person in your pursuers path is sometimes warranted.

I have field-tested these items. They can work well in real battles. But once again, don't wait until you are attacked to discover how you might use such weapons effectively. *Practice beforehand.*

PRINCIPLES OF OPEN-HANDED
BLOCKING TECHNIQUES

I have mentioned that I do not strike to the hard bones of the head with a closed fist (unless I have a glove on). Now here's a big flash for you taekwon-do people. I never use a closed-hand block in a real fight, either.

Sure, wado ryu uses blocks like taekwon-do's *chukyo marki* (rising block). So do most karate styles. Nonetheless, it doesn't matter if you give the moves Korean or Japanese names, they still don't work very well in real fights. They are too slow as well as having some other real disadvantages.

Try to follow this, people, because it is one of the most fundamentally important concepts to understand in order for you to avoid being punched out (read *knocked out*) at the very outset of the attack.

An open-handed block is more properly termed a parry. It moves faster than a closed fist because a closed fist puts tension in the muscles that an open hand does not. This tension slows your movement down. Besides, you do not need a fist to intercept a blow. Many times you don't even need a fist to strike a blow. So why slow yourself down with a clenched fist at the end of your arm?

Some traditionalists will say, "The fist creates the power necessary to block the more powerful strikes. It is not always needed, but some attacks demand this type of block." My response is, "Not in my fighting experience."

The idea of blocking means arresting or stopping a motion. This is a mistake in itself. You do not want to arrest your opponent's forward motion; you only want to avoid being hit. You don't want to throw up a rigid arm and block; you want to slip the blow. You want to slightly deflect it which, when combined with a slight movement of the target (your head), makes the blow just miss you.

Anybody who has developed any real fighting skill or is experienced in full-contact karate or boxing knows this. The best counterstrikes occur when the opponent's blow comes close to actually hitting you but misses. This way, you are there with the counterpunch while he is still moving forward and into your blow. Open-handed slips/blocks achieve this the best. Boxers achieve it with the bob-and-weave combined with the counterpunch. Boxers can be difficult opponents indeed.

There is another central advantage to open-handed parries over arresting-power blocks. In real fights, you are most likely going to be ambushed, which means the opening shot has a good chance of landing if you aren't fast enough. A rising block or any kind of arresting-motion block is not likely to be fast enough. When such a block fails, all the linear geometry of classic karate stances will only ensure that you receive the full power of the attacker's blow. A horse stance, for example, will just make you less mobile and more likely to be hit again.

It is true that if you can pull off a closed-fist arresting-motion block combined with the classic ripostes, then you will probably do some first-class rib cracking on your attacker. But chances are you won't pull off a rising block in a real fight unless you are very good. This means very fast and very well trained.

Consequently, I feel these blocks are too dangerous to try in real fights. They leave you exposed and immobile should they fail. And if they fail, they fail completely, just as when they succeed, they can succeed completely.

There will be a few well-schooled martial arts people out there who realize that a rising block as performed by most martial artists is not the correct form of the technique. Further, they will understand that by just watching someone throw a rising block in the air, it is very difficult to distinguish common mistakes from proper form. These people will realize that the movement I am about to describe is an example of what a proper rising-type block can achieve in an actual combat situation, even though the form I will describe is quite different from a traditional rising or forearm block.

I am not going to complicate my book with a diatribe on this. I just threw in the above paragraph so you ranking black belts would know that I realize what you might be thinking. Thus, you don't have to grind your teeth while reading this, wanting to yell, "Yeah, damn it, but that's because so few people understand this basic technique and can execute it properly. It isn't supposed to fully arrest motion and take the full power on the arm." Okay, I said it for you. Feel better now?

It is true; few people, even plenty of shodans I have

seen, fully understand or execute a simple rising block with perfection. So maybe this means that it is not so simple to do this way?

For you people who want to know what the hell I'm talking about, go watch Fumio Demura execute a rising block. You likely won't see the difference, but there is a big one. Mainly, he does it right because he is a master. But once again, if one has to become a master to make a technique work in a real combat situation, how useful is the technique for most people?

The approach that I have found very useful has the advantage that if the slip block is a little late or not quite in perfect position, it still keeps you from receiving the brunt of a well-focused blow. It is only the really well-focused, full-on shots that will knock out most people when executed by the average attacker. Anything less will give you a chance to recover and defend yourself.

What you must do is spoil the focus of the blow. This is easier to accomplish than it first may seem. It is always easier to screw something up than it is to do something perfectly. Basically, you are just screwing up your attacker's blow. You are ruining its energy-transfer potential by getting something in the way before it lands.

Think about the candle drill. If you learn to put the candle out with an acceleration blow, then you have achieved good focus. But consider this: if someone taps your hand very slightly on the way to the candle, it would be all but impossible to put it out. The focus is broken. Now, when someone swings at your head and you can get your hand in the way, you can break the focus of his blow such that the energy transfer is substantially degraded and you don't absorb the full force. You may get hit, maybe even see some stars, but you won't take the full force, thus giving you a decent chance to recover.

The method I will put forth to achieve this is one I have used in every fight I have ever been in that involved somebody punching at me, once I learned that it could work in a real fight. I think it is a simple concept to grasp, and most people can learn the technique to some degree of effectiveness with only a moderate amount of practice. It can also be continually perfected and economized to the point where it can have a remarkable effect when executed properly. Finally, it is a technique that can be generalized to various forms of attack once it is truly and conceptually understood.

Closing the Gate

For any strike to connect, it must trace a given path to the target. The path depends on the type of strike, be it a

The next three photos only show the mechanics of the outside crane; distances are not meant to be realistic. In this photo, the open hand moves up to catch the incoming blow at the opponent's wrist. This gives the tactile feel that instantly tells the defender which way and how much to move the target (his head) out of the attack line so the blow just misses.

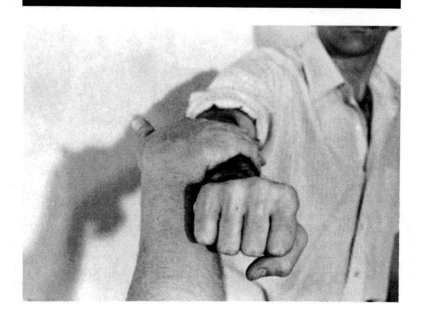

Simultaneously, the defender's hand turns on its own axis and displaces the punch slightly to the right (top left). The attacker's blow is thus slightly deflected from the original attack line. Avoid trying to achieve this by pushing away the attacker's arm with force, as this would be contesting the opponent's power. That won't work in a real fight if your attacker is significantly stronger than you.

Here the execution of the outside crane has been performed well, which allows the final "pat down" of the blow (bottom left). Note how this hand motion follows directly from the previous photo, another example of economy of movement.

hook, straight punch, or even backfist or vertical fist. It also depends on where the target is (height, distance, etc.).

In a dynamic situation, it can be very tricky to follow the path of a blow and intercept it before it hits you because it moves so fast and is hard to see coming most of the time. But think about this. To hurt you it has to hit you and to hit you on, for example, the left side of your head, there is a point along its path within your space that it must pass through before it connects. I call this the "gate." This is a critical concept so listen up.

You can always know instantly where this gate is located in relation to your own body, just as you can always put your hand on your forehead or nose, even in a totally dark room. You don't need visual cues to do this. In a sense, therefore, you don't really need to see the punch to block it. With some practice you can instantly perceive the type of blow about to be delivered or already on its way and simply "close the gate" it must pass through to hit you. It is not necessary to truly be "faster" than your attacker to achieve this.

The method below allows you to almost always intercept some portion of the strike, even if it partially lands. Like I said, this breaks its true power. This interception will be done with an open hand. You will learn how it works by doing the perception drills with training partners.

THE OUTSIDE CRANE

Keep in mind that I don't claim to be a master of anything and I am not putting forth any "system" of martial art. What I am trying to get across is some moves that have worked for me in real fights on numerous occasions.

Direct your attention to the photos. One of the things you have to realize about photos in a book that describe a self-defense or martial arts technique is that for the pictures to show you anything, *the distance between the opponents is often exaggerated.* Otherwise, you wouldn't see anything but two people jammed up next to each other with their hands obscured by their bodies. For this reason, the photos here exaggerate the distance between the opponents as well.

Consider the first close-up photo of hand position for the outside crane technique (page 99). Here, the defender's open hand has moved up to "close the gate," which the attacker's blow must pass through in order to land properly. In this case, the blow is the straight punch and the target is the defender's face.

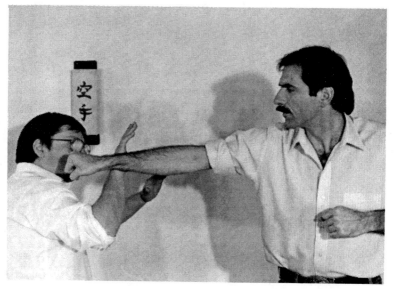

Here's the outside crane from a different perspective. At this point the defender's hand has already caught the attacker's wrist and has made the turn on its own axis, displacing the blow from the original attack line. Note that otherwise the blow would have already landed since it is past the defender's head. Also notice that the defender's left hand is moving to the outside of the attacker's elbow to further lock out the new attack angle.

The defender has now engaged the "pat down" with his right hand while his left locks out the attacker's shot at the outside of the elbow (top left). The attacker's forward motion is continued rather than arrested by these actions, drawing him into the defender's counterstrike.

Here, the counterstrike is the rising vertical fist to the nose (bottom left). Note how the attacker has been pulled slightly forward and has lost some balance. He would have to recover his balance before being able to offer any type of defense. The defender gives him no such opportunity since the vertical fist has been chambered by his evasion of the attacker's strike. Thus, the evasion of the blow and the counterstrike are truly one! Study all three photos in sequence and appreciate the continuous "flow" of things.

The moment the attacker's hand makes contact with the defender's hand, and it must in order to land, the defender feels this contact and instantly turns his hand, as seen in the second photo. In fact, the defender should begin this turn just before first contact so that the attacker's hand strikes something that is already moving, which tends to deflect the path of the attacker's blow away from the line it must follow to connect with the defender's face.

Compare the close-up photos with the corresponding full-frame photos that follow. Note that the defender, having felt contact with the incoming blow and having previously perceived the path of the attacker's strike, has dropped his head slightly away from the line of attack. At this point, but for the interception of the blow and the resulting slight deflection combined with the slight dropping away of the head, the strike would have already connected, as the punch has passed the defender's head. This is true even though the distance between the two combatants is exaggerated in the photos (they are further apart than they would likely be in a real fight).

In the second close-up photo, the defender's hand has rotated on its own axis. It is not really trying to push the strike away—that would be contesting the attacker's power, which is something we always try to avoid. You can see that the displacement of the attacker's blow away from its original path is effected by this turn of the defender's wrist.

You would ideally like this interception to occur as far from the target (your face) as possible without having to reach out to intercept. Keep in mind you are just closing the gate when your hand goes up there. It really is happening too fast for you to do anything else. However, despite the speed of events, you are (by virtue of your training) perceptually prepared to turn the opponent's blow and move your head out of the strike path in a single, coordinated movement. This means the two actions basically become one movement. This is called *unity of movement*.

Finally, consider the third close-up photo. Here, the defender's hand has continued its turn until the palm is on top of the punching arm and the fingers have a slight "hold" on the shot. This is *never* a grab. A grab demands muscular tension that would slow this move down to the point where it could never work. (In this case, the attacker's blow was somewhat overextended in the first place. This does happen in real fights, as the sucker puncher tends to overcommit his opening shot because he is confident it will land. Every fighter doesn't do this, but we will return to the more skillful adversary a bit later.)

This slight palm-down position on the attacker's incoming wrist or arm allows the defender to further direct an already moving object. The idea now is not to move it so much in the horizontal plane such as the wrist turn achieved, but to direct the blow downward along the natural path of gravity. Your hand remains in contact with the blow, drawing it down and towards you but slightly to the side and thus out of the way.

If an attacker telegraphs his strike and also overextends, it is often possible to combine this redirection downward with a checking of the attacker's elbow with the defender's other hand. In this case, there are two points of contact that the defender has on the attacker's arm. This gives ideal redirection potential, and the check on the attacker's elbow locks out the joint, ensuring control over the path of the incoming strike.

Of course, all this doesn't work perfectly every time. Nothing does in real fights. But it will likely never work if you don't practice it. Let me point out, however, that when I have used this reasonably simple move alone against overcommitted attacks, it has made the attacker fall straight into the floor with no other assistance from me. Most times, though, it won't go so sweetly, and a follow-up strike to the nose or elbow to the throat will be called for.

Any part of the outside crane that you execute, even if you don't have time to complete the whole maneuver, will still help you a lot. Just the initial contact with the wrist and following the blow in with that hand will be a real plus in telling your body how to move your head away as well as robbing the shot of its best power.

Finally, observe in the third full-frame photo the formation of the vertical fist to the opponent's nose after drawing down his strike. Keep in mind that since the forward motion of the attacker has not been arrested (as would be the case with a rising block), he is basically hurling himself into the defender's blow. An alternative strike from your toolbox would be the horizontal elbow or open-hand shot to the throat.

The Importance of Facing

Facing is another element to consider with the outside crane. We will consider two basic facing positions: inside gate and outside gate. In the previous example, the defender was at his attacker's outside gate—that is, the defender was positioned outside of the attacker's arm. If you are facing squarely with your enemy such that you are between his two arms, then you are at the inside gate.

The outside gate is the preferred position because the attacker's other hand is not in a good position for a quick and effective follow-up blow. He would have to cross himself, which doesn't work, or turn his body and withdraw the first striking arm before he can strike with his other hand. This takes too much time, as you will already be on him with stunning blows before he even realizes his first strike had failed.

Conversely, if you are at the inside gate when you slip his first blow, then you will probably be the object of an immediate strike with the other hand. This is the old one/two punch. We are going to see how to deal with this situation when we look at the inside crane.

Your opponent is more likely to throw a straight punch rather than a hook when you are at his outside gate, whereas the hook is more likely than the straight punch when you're at the inside gate. Of course, you should not interpret my statement to mean that only the hook will be thrown from the inside gate or that the straight punch is thrown exclusively from the outside gate. Anything can happen in real fights, but I have observed that this relationship between a given gate and a given blow occurs frequently enough to be useful for training purposes.

The Quality of Your Opposition

Some of you are thinking, "Shit, if the guy throws that sloppy a shot from that long a range and as over-committed as pictured here, why would I even need to defend against it? Why not just casually step out of the way and go home for a pizza?"

Your point is well taken, but if you feel this way, it is probably because you are a student or instructor of martial arts. Therefore you are used to people throwing reasonably controlled shots, even though you have seen some sloppy, overextended strikes in the dojo, especially during free sparring when people get a little excited.

Well, dear reader, as a general rule, people get real excited in real fights and they do throw overextended shots with some frequency. There are a number of reasons for this, and I'll eventually run a few of the more important ones past you, *but do not take what I am saying here to mean that you can safely underestimate the sucker puncher or streetfighter!* As I pointed out in Chapter 2, the untrained fighter has a lot going for him.

Nonetheless, without the benefit of proper training, the more power the average guy tries to put in a blow, the more overextended it often becomes. Consider the mind-set of the sucker puncher. He is attacking by ambush. He knows he has to close the distance fast before his victim is alerted so he will try to land the most powerful shot he can with this opening blow. This often means a somewhat overextended blow.

Since most people are not real *aware*, and the sucker puncher has likely concluded his interview and selected the proper victim, his ambush works most of the time. This guy doesn't try to improve on or change something that has worked for him in the past, which is why the barroom warrior so often leads with his right hand and overextends the blow. Think about it.

Every now and then I had to deal with somebody who had more formal or effective training in hand-to-hand fighting. Most of the time they were boxers. Only very few times did they seem to be students of an Asian system. (Having watched every Bruce Lee movie or a string of "Kung Fu" episodes does not make one a student of an Asian system. Plenty of dildos who have never seen the inside of a dojo or kwoon will try to throw a kick to your head or some other la-la land version of Asian fighting techniques. I don't count these nerds.) I like to think that true Asian-style fighters do not cause much trouble because people who stay with such systems long enough to know how to use them often develop more mature attitudes toward barroom brawling. Namely, they don't get involved if there is a reasonable alternative.

A decent boxer does not overextend his attack. He often knows how to move and hit and can be a formidable opponent. When he throws a punch, it is returned as quickly as it went out. There is very little chance of capturing his striking wrist with the pat-down portion of the outside crane. Furthermore, the boxer is a counterpuncher and combination puncher.

The first objective of defense against a more polished assailant remains the same: don't get hit. Against the better fighter, especially one who attacks from ambush, you will have only a split second to engage any defensive move. The open-handed interception is faster than any other form, making it more likely to get a piece of an incoming blow regardless of how well the blow is executed by your attacker. The faster he is, the more you need the open-hand approach to avoid his blow.

Another advantage of the open hand is that it is much more sensitive to the enemy's movements than is a closed fist. With practice, just having the open hand up and slapping it against a blow that partially, though not perfectly, connects will let you know which way to move to escape or check the next shot. Things move so fast in a real fight that having a hand on your opponent may become your primary cue to which way he is moving. This tactile feeling will also "tell" you where the targets are for the counterstrike. Visual cues alone aren't always adequate when everything is moving in a blur. This is especially true if you have been partially stunned by your opponent's blow.

A third advantage of the open hand is that, if you practice the movement, you can often get the return strike (vertical fist, throat shot, etc.) because it follows so directly from the slip, even on boxers.

I will return to this subject of dealing with boxers and other more skilled opponents. For now, however, we need to proceed to more fundamental defensive techniques. Suffice to say that boxers are tough opponents and I have generally dealt with them by going directly to a grappling situation where I could use simple throws, head butts, and elbow and knee strikes while I tied up the his best weapons—a pair of fast, coordinated hands.

THE INSIDE CRANE

The inside crane is used to defend against strikes when you are at your opponent's inside gate between his

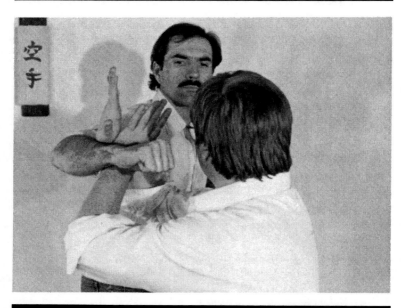

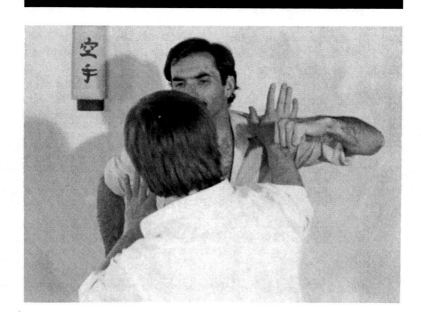

Here we see the inside crane defense during the instant of contact (top left). This is a defense against a right hook to the head, one of the most common in the saloon fighter's repertoire. Note that the defender's right hand is closest to the attacker (strong-side-forward facing) while his left is at the attacker's right wrist. He could execute the shuto to the attacker's neck with his right (lead) hand directly from this position without changing hand position or anything else. Again, the evasion of the blow and the chambering of the counterstrike are one movement.

When defending from the inside gate, you must be immediately aware of the attacker's other hand. In this photo, the defender's right hand has not gone to the aforementioned shuto to the neck because he felt the attacker pulling away his right hand, which must precede the throwing of the left (bottom left). Perceiving this body movement, the defender instinctively checks the left hook with a "source block" at the attacker's left shoulder. This is accompanied by an evasive head movement.

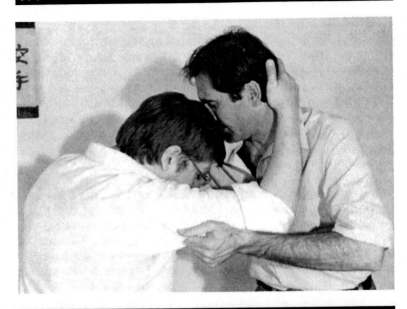

In this case, after checking the left hook at the shoulder, the front head butt follows (top left). Note how the defender's hand slipped behind the attacker's head directly from the shoulder. In actual practice, however, I have more often used the open-handed throat shot or the palm-heel strike. The front head butt is quite useful when grappling.

You must practice defending from the ground because in real fights, the battle often goes to the ground, especially after some grappling occurs. Here we see the shuto to the attacker's neck (bottom left). This is the blow that would have followed directly from the inside crane in the previous sequence had it not been necessary to check the left hook at the shoulder instead. This blow should be a series of strikes that alternate from the right side of the neck to the left in a fast and focused manner. Be alert for the escape when your opponent is stunned. An elbow strike to the throat can also work well here. You sometimes need to grab his hair and pull him down into your elbow.

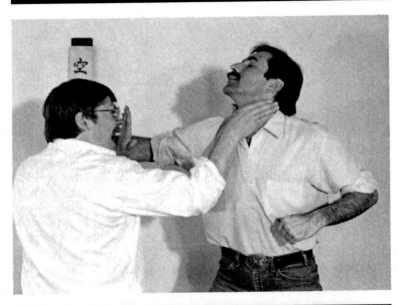

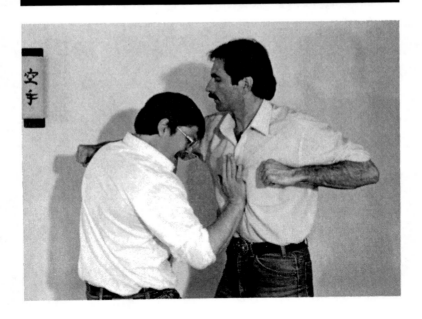

The open-handed throat shot following the moment of contact of an inside crane defense (top left). This is a strong alternative to the shuto to the neck after checking the right hook. Throat shots are generally very disabling when they land.

The palm-heel to the solar plexus is another good strike that follows from the inside crane (bottom left). It is not as incapacitating as a good throat shot, but in real fights the blows must simply "flow," and this one has flowed for me real well.

arms. As pointed out before, the hook to the head is the most common shot when you are at the inside gate.

In the first photo on page 112, we see the inside crane at the instant of impact with the opponent's right hook. Note that the defender's right hand is closest to the attacker while his left hand is at the attacker's wrist. Also observe that the defender's two hands are touching each other at or near the wrist. The defender has moved his head into his attacker to make the target too close for the point of focus that the attacker had in mind.

Suppose the defender could only get his right hand up to deflect the opponent's blow. This would help, but the strike could still slip around the gate and land with unacceptable power. Now think about what would happen if the defender only had his left hand at the attacker's wrist. This would help because the defender could still turn the wrist and deflect the blow similar to the outside crane, but the blow still could land with too much of its original power. However, when the two hands come together simultaneously at the correct gate position, then the defender is fairly safe from receiving a full-force shot.

Remember, the head moves inside the blow concurrent with the technique. By combining the two movements, each reinforces the other and the blow cannot easily slip around the defense, making it very difficult for the blow to land with any decisive power. All this is combined with a slight rotation of the body away from the path of the blow and a slight step toward the attacker.

Once the hook is intercepted, you have to counterattack immediately. The shuto to the side of the attacker's exposed neck is a natural response, as it is already chambered at high gate. It should follow instantly after the attacker's blow is defeated. The shuto can be followed up with a palm heel or throat shot.

Since you are at the inside gate, you must be aware of

the possibility of the opponent's other hand landing a blow immediately after the first shot is checked. Even though all this happens in a split second, your hands will instantly feel the first striking arm pull away should it begin to do so. Your opponent has to withdraw this arm in order to execute a second attack with the other hand.

If you sense this, instead of throwing the shuto, your hand goes directly to the opponent's opposite shoulder as you move your body into him. The result is his blow never generates full force and may fail to connect with the target entirely, as your head has moved inside the blow's range.

This technique, when properly executed, sets your man up like a tin can on a fence, a fish in a barrel, a duck in repose . . . you get the idea. This is because when he throws the first shot and it does not connect solidly, and he then throws the other and it too is partially arrested from its intended path, there is a moment when he can't do anything but stand there somewhat flat-footed. A moment is a long time in an actual fight. Since your open hands are still moving freely, you flow into the next technique from your tool box. The vertical fist is a natural from the inside gate position. As mentioned, the palm-heel strike and throat shot work well here, too.

With a very fast right hook, you may only get your left hand on the incoming shot (or vice-versa if it's a left hook). If this is all you get on it, but you still move your head away and inside with correct timing, then the blow should not put you away unless the guy happens to be Conan the Barbarian.

I said nothing works perfectly all the time. Once a Conan-type threw a good fast hook to my head, but I managed to get both my hands up and together to close the gate. However, his power was such that it blasted my own hands into my head. Still, if I'd not executed the move, I'd have definitely been put out like a light. Though stunned, I instinctively moved in where those monster hooks would not be so dangerous. I blasted him with some reverse punches to his midsection, which had no effect at all. It sort of felt like hitting the heavy bag, only this guy's gut was a bit harder on my hands. It was definitely one of those "go for the escape" situations.

UNIFYING CONCEPTS OF
THE INSIDE AND OUTSIDE CRANES

The inside and outside cranes are useful in real fights because I have used them in real fights enough to know. Experiment with them in the drills. Understand that your objective is to strip away all excess movements that complicate or slow down the technique.

Notice how both techniques can be seen as no more than just throwing your hands up to avoid being hit in the face. Basically that's all they are because it is a natural motion and therefore easier to execute spontaneously in a real attack. The movement has simply been refined to redirect the line of the incoming blow and to set up the counterstrike.

Relaxation

Just as in delivering a blow, avoiding an opponent's blow demands a relaxed mind which does not impart muscular tension to your limbs. Think about the expression "scared stiff." When you are afraid, the natural tendency is to tense muscles. If you are scared stiff, the muscles are so tensed that you can't move at all. Therefore the first common element to these defensive techniques is *relaxation*. Avoid tension in the arm and hand as it moves up to intercept the blow. Just using an open hand instead of a closed hand facilitates this relaxation.

Economy of Movement

Never reach out to "block." Make the minimum movement necessary to slip the blow and redirect it.

Here is a way to get an idea of how far you can reach out to close the gate. Hold out the little finger and thumb of one hand so they are spread the maximum distance apart. Place the thumb against your body (about in the middle of the bottom rib toward the defending arm) and the little finger against the bent elbow of your defending arm. Your elbow should not move much farther from your body than this when slipping a blow. By much farther, I mean three to four inches. This is a basic rule of thumb—there's always some lanky types who can safely reach a little farther.

Unity of Movement

Learn to coordinate into one motion your hand moving up and your head moving away. The hand can be considered an insect antenna that tells you the direction of the blow without having to think about it. This allows your head to move out of the way without having to think about it. With training, *these two actions become one.* It is like putting your hand on a hot stove. You don't think about it; your hand instantly pops off the hot surface even if you did not see the stove before you set your hand down. When you've developed some unity with these movements, your head will instinctively pop away in the right direction just enough to slip the blow according to the felt impact of your hand on the attacker's strike.

Avoid Contesting the Opponent's Power

This is important primarily because if he is stronger than you, you will be overcome. We do not try to stop the incoming blow; we simply make it miss its target. Not only is this a lot easier to achieve but it keeps your opponent moving into your counterstrike. It also makes it more difficult for him to immediately launch another attack because the first one is still underway as far as his mind and body are concerned.

CONTINUOUS ATTACK

The next defense concept we will look at is one we have touched on already: continuous attack. The idea should be fairly easy to grasp at this point. Like the crane defenses, continuous attack demands the integration of relaxation, economy and unity of movement, and not contesting the opponent's power so you can flow from one item in your toolbox to the next.

When you land a blow, it is because the opponent was unable to defend against it the instant before it landed. How effectively can he defend against a second blow the instant after the first one lands? The answer is, not too well. Extend this line of logic to the third, fourth, and fifth blows.

In short, if you have developed the skills mentioned above, you should be able to immediately follow up with several shots after you hit your man with one good shot. Each successive shot should be more damaging than the last so the enemy is given no chance to recover.

Remember, getting in that first good shot from ambush and following up with more shots so the victim never has a chance to defend himself is the basic tactic of the sucker puncher. Though it works fairly well for most sucker punchers, it will work better for you because you will have a better grasp of the principle. The trick is to first slip the sucker puncher's opening shot or you will not get a chance to apply any other technique in your defense.

Study the photographs of the escape from a front choke (pages 47-54). I chose this particular sequence because it displays all the aforementioned fundamental elements of defense with the unifying theme of continuous attack. The photo captions address the mechanics of the techniques. But notice how the *concepts* display themselves. In the first frame, the choke is not directly resisted. I do not try to grab his arms and pull them off, as this would be contesting the attacker's power. The guy still is choking me as I deliver the first blow, the elbow strike, which he is completely unable to avoid or block.

If he continues holding onto your throat, simply continue with the elbow strike. Do not go from one strike to another simply to demonstrate your varied arsenal or to offer a crowd-pleasing display. You go from one type of blow to another when the former blow sets up the next more powerful technique. Should the guy still hang on to your throat after being hit with the elbow, that's fine. The dude's either out on his feet or is just real stupid. Therefore, there is no better shot than another elbow to the neck. Deliver it as many times as required.

In the photos, the attacker does the more natural thing and begins to pull away from me. The natural transition from the elbow is to grab the back of his head for the head/wrist spin (which we will look at later), a good example of economy of movement. This sets up the knee to the solar plexus. We go to the solar plexus because we are bound to get him somewhere in the midsection. It's a pretty big target. Now, having delivered the knee strike, the opponent is doubled over and incapacitated. This gives us the extra second to go for a little more accuracy in our next shot, the knee to the face. Notice the unity of movement here—the hand on the head is coordinated with the rising knee strike.

The knee to the face has all but finished the guy, but for good measure we give him the old favorite as he falls away, the shuto to the neck. This blow follows because our hand has bounced up off the top of the guy's head when our knee impacted with his face. Again, we see an open hand at high gate becoming a shuto to the opponent's neck, another example of economy of movement.

Now consider the generalization of this particular chaining of moves from a different starting point. Instead of a choke, imagine we were at the point where some basic grappling was going on. Alternatively, suppose I'd just slipped a hook shot with an inside crane, blocked a follow-up strike from his opposite hand at the source (his shoulder), and executed a palm-heel strike to his solar plexus. Any of these scenarios could lead directly to this entire sequence of continuous attack.

Do not forget, however, that your objective is to get away unhurt. You generally want to disengage from a substantially larger and stronger opponent and escape rather than continue with a series of blows with the objective of dropping your man. In general, though, once is not enough. Even if you want to escape, you likely will best be served by throwing a minimum of two or three shots before the break away.

USING COMMON SENSE IN YOUR TACTICS

In the sequence I show here, the opponent, though taller and with greater arm reach, is not a larger-boned person than I. Notice that I am fighting him inside his reach. If he were a good boxer and got away from me, he might land some combinations. I can't allow this, and since he isn't a whole lot bigger or stronger, I chose the tactics you see here because I have confidence in their success. The guy is not so big that I can't hurt him.

However, if the guy were just as tall (in this case about 6'1"; I am 5'10") but was a 245-pounder and built like a linebacker for the Dallas Cowboys, then I would try another approach, namely to stun and escape. It would be harder for me to get the guy moving like the previous scenario because the blows wouldn't hurt him as much, and it would be more difficult to bend over his body as well. He could recover, and then I could be in real trouble.

Therefore, learn to instantly size up your opponent's body type. If you get a chance to see him before the attack (*awareness*), pay particular note to his features. How thick are his wrists? This is a good indicator of bone size since even if the guy has a lot of extra weight and maybe looks big, this wrist size remains constant. Similarly, scan his head. How far apart are the eyes? How thick is his neck? How tall is he? What do you think he tips the scales at? All of this will dictate the best tactics to use if you tangle with the guy. Practice this by sizing people up in the street, at the grocery store, and so forth. Learn to instantly recognize how big somebody really is.

Fat guys sometimes act big and maybe have good-sized bones, but they don't often last long in a fight before they run out of gas. Thus you may want to stay away from them and make them move around a lot as they try to connect with a punch or grapple with you. When they are breathing hard, then start to work on them if the situation demands it. Don't make the mistake of thinking fat guys are always slow. They are not always slow, especially before they get tired.

Another thing I have noticed about pounding on fat guys. Sometimes they can't take a blow to the head very well. I think this may be because the fat guys who have forced me to defend myself, especially when working as a bouncer, were used to relying on their obvious size to intimidate their opponents. They didn't have much fight experience because people did not usually call them out and mix it up with them. The result—they never learned how to take a punch.

This could be second guessing on my part. Who knows? But here is something I do know. Getting hit in the head a few times helps you get used to functioning with a stunned mind and foggy vision. Boxers are often good at this because of their full-contact training methods. Also, even a big guy can be hurt by punches to his face. The face is pretty sensitive, especially the nose.

KEEPING YOUR EYES OPEN

This idea of keeping your eyes open in a fight might seem obvious to you, but if I were to identify the single most common error made by people in their attempts to defend themselves, I would probably pick their failure to keep their eyes on the opponent.

In every sport their is a maxim such as, "Keep your eye on the ball!" This maxim applies to real fighting twice over. The problem is, in sports the ball isn't trying to punch you in the head; in a fight your opponent most certainly will be. Because of this, people tend to put their head down so as not to expose it. This often occurs after a few of their attacker's blows have landed.

This is a very big mistake. When you put your head down, you cannot see your opponent's blows, let alone his preparation for the blow. This makes it more difficult to slip or otherwise avoid the power of those shots, to say the very least. If you can control distance with a good slipping-back retreat, then you should be able to keep your head erect and eyes on everything your opponent is trying to do.

Again, we are dealing with a principle that must be experienced in free-sparring training. In particular, when you're using head gear and blows to the head are permitted, stop and think after you really get hit hard in the head. You may discover that your head was down and you could not see the blow coming.

When you first concentrate on keeping your head up and eyes open, you may get hit even more during free sparring. This is temporary! You are just learning how to do it so expect to get hit at this point. Learn this idea in your free-sparring training with head gear *before* you get in a real balls-to-the-wall streetfight.

Boxers will duck their heads, but all the good ones do so with proper timing while keeping a good eye on their opponent. Actually, boxing is a good training method to learn how to keep your head up while ducking and slipping blows with upper trunk movements. But be warned: with all its strong points, Western boxing is "overly daring because of the restrictions on illegal moves." (Bruce Lee, from his book, *The Tao of Jeet Kune Do*.)

I've seen very few fights where one guy was a trained boxer and totally outclassed his opponent. There was one such incident that occurred about seven years ago that stands out in my mind.

After slipping the sucker punch with an upper trunk movement (ducking or slipping, I didn't see), the boxer moved away from his man and assumed a boxing stance. He was dancing up on his toes, throwing fake punches, bobbing and weaving, the whole nine yards, from a distance where neither man could land a blow. Then the boxer stepped in quickly and landed two snappy lefts followed by a more powerful right to the guy's jaw. He stepped back as if to survey the damage, then stepped back in and started working on the guy's body with nice reverse punches. Again he stepped back, but this time he landed a right hook on the way out.

His opponent was totally outclassed. I was not working in this bar and was really surprised that the owners let this thing go on so long. Either the place had no bouncer or the guy was taking a shit, because a bunch of the locals finally called the show off before any more punches were thrown. The sucker puncher definitely got more than he had bargained for and was bleeding a bit, but that's about all.

I certainly would not criticize the boxer's show, but it is not my personal style to handle things like this. I never stop to survey the damage as long as my opponent is still on his feet. I want to get it done with as quick as possible because the longer it lasts, the more chance I have of getting hurt. Still, this little pugilistic demonstration once again showed me that there is more than one way to skin a cat, so to speak. The boxer was smaller boned but a little taller than the guy he was punching on. He did not seem to hurt his hands as far as I could tell.

I think it was the boxer's confidence in his ability and physical conditioning as well as his actual training experience that allowed him to control and defeat his man. He kept his head erect the whole time, even when he did his little "Hey look, I'm a boxer" number with the bobbing and weaving bit. He defeated the ambush, and after all, that's all that really counts.

BLOW PERCEPTION AND
ANGLE OF ATTACK DRILLS

While there are many types of punches, the ones you are most likely to be attacked with are the overhead right and the hook. You would do well to practice defending against these two blows before trying to generalize the crane techniques to other types of shots.

Draw a chalk line or run a line of masking tape on the floor. Face your training partner with the line running between both your legs at a distance a bit more than his arm's length away from you. This means he will have to advance slightly in order to land a powerful shot to your head, if this were his actual intent.

With the puncher remaining on the line, take up various positions to the left and right, but always keep the same distance apart. In slow motion, have your partner throw either the right hook or overhead right to your head. This will allow you to see the difference in the angles of attack and how your attacker must move to throw these two blows depending on how you're facing him.

Observe the cues your partner gives as he initiates a punch from his side. Most people will give plenty of obvious cues here, including the shoulder drop on the side of the punching hand, the hand tensing, sometimes abruptly stopping his forward motion before uncorking the blow. (I believe it was Hollywood Bob, an aikido man, who said, " . . . the body tells.") Only a good fighter has managed to train them away. (Do you see what is meant by speed being achieved by stripping away excess motion rather than simply going faster? When all excess motion is gone, the cues pretty much disappear, too.)

The more subtle cues, which can best be appreciated through experience, are seen in the eyes and face. These cues will vary from individual to individual. Some will stare right into your eyes trying to "project" on you, sometimes scanning for a cue of fear before launching the punch. At the other end of the spectrum, some will pretend to turn away from you when actually they are winding up the shot.

When someone is moving up on you, possibly to throw a punch, the first thing you might do is "move to the corner." This means, at the least, stepping off the imaginary centerline and moving slightly back at an angle. This can be done without making a big defensive show of it. It will force the guy coming toward you to tip his hand if he does intend to strike you because he must shift his facing to maintain his attack angle. You will be able to perceive his intentions much more easily when you force him to draw out the cues like that. The line drill gives you some idea what those cues are as far as his gate, movement of his shoulders in the gate, orientation of his hips, and the state of his hands (open or closing to a fist, tensed or relaxed, etc.).

Try this drill where the distance between you and your partner starts out far enough for you to move to the corner as he steps towards you and delivers the mock blow. Note his shifts in facing and the cues that precede these shifts. It helps to have different people throwing the shot because different people with different body types will display a different set of cues.

Next, close the distance to where the opponent is standing so close that the hook is about the only blow he can use. You should only see his face and most of his shoulders. To get the correct distance, place your elbows against the side of your body and hold your forearm straight out with fingers outstretched until you can touch your opponent.

The idea here is to reduce the set of cues to the ones available after the opponent has closed on you. In a real fight, you may have an adrenaline rush that gives you more raw speed and power than you may have previously experienced. But without a visual, physical, tactile, or other cue/stimulus to tell your body (not your conscious mind) how to respond, the adrenaline may only help you take a shot without being put away. Your objective is to imprint these cues in your subconscious so your body moves with that extra speed and power such that you avoid the shot altogether or substantially reduce its effectiveness. To do this, you have to train to perceive the cues, which will give you that advance notice of the blow and its angle of attack.

Finally, try this close-up drill where you only look into the guy's eyes and must rely on peripheral vision alone to catch the body cues.

When you work on these drills, keep a relaxed but attentive mind. Don't allow any horseplay. Keep a reasonably serious attitude while training. Periodically during the training session, stop and evaluate what is happening. What's working, what's not, and why? Test your hypotheses in continued drills.

Repeat the drills very slowly at first. Remember, he is not going to hit you so relax and devote your exclusive attention to perceiving the cues. When you feel you have at least identified the cues, then experiment with the "Zen gaze." I think I just made this term up, but some people will know what I refer to. (Right, Eagle?)

The Zen gaze is where, to the outside observer, you seem to be almost staring off into space. In reality, you have expanded your field of vision such that you don't allow yourself to focus on any one thing. You are using peripheral vision in a new, more sophisticated way. The purpose of experimenting with this expanded visual perception is that it can allow you to catch visual cues at the periphery of your normal vision in an everyday situation that you otherwise might not "see." This could allow you to catch a glimpse of that blindside sucker punch on the way in, or maybe even a body cue that is a precursor to the actual blow. (You can afford to experiment with this in the drill, but not in a real fight!)

My aikido pals, including Eagle and Hollywood, might say that this gaze can be used in actual combat against multiple attackers as they circle you for position. I say, "Hell! If you can really handle multiple attackers (without any sort of weapon) like this, then your shit wouldn't stink either!" Against several circling assailants, I wouldn't even wait for their attack. I'd take the battle to them by opening a door with a preemptive strike to make my escape. I'm not saying Eagle or Hollywood couldn't pull off their tactics in such a situation. Just remember, they have studied and practiced this aikido stuff for years.

When doing these perception drills, be careful! I know a lot of people will end up punching each other out by accident. Don't be one of them. This means don't exceed your ability. First do them right, then gradually increase the speed of the strikes. If you have developed some focus control with the striking drills (candles, cloth, etc.), you and your partner should be able to stop a blow just before it lands.

The best way to practice an activity is to participate in the activity itself. Unfortunately, there really is no practical way to practice real fighting by real fighting. This is partly why a lot of martial systems can get so far removed from the reality of combat.

OUTSIDE CRANE DRILLS

The outside crane is used primarily on the straight punch. At first, know beforehand the type of blow coming in while you train. Later we'll mix them up.

Drill One: Mechanics of the Outside Crane

With your partner throwing a straight punch to your head in slow motion, *mirror* his speed and execute a full outside crane. Raise your open hand to close the gate that the punch must pass through to connect. Your wrist will meet his simultaneously.

He continues the slow-motion punch as your wrist rotates on its own axis, which will displace his blow by a distance about the width of your wrist (refer back to the photos). As you make contact and your wrist turns, you should be drawing the blow slightly inward and downward. At the same time, your head is dropping out of the line of attack.

Note how your hand on his incoming blow tells you which way and how much to drop your head. From time to time, close your eyes once you make contact so that the only cue you have as to the line of his attack—and thus how to move your head away properly—is the feeling of your hand on his wrist.

Occasionally, perform these drills so slowly that it takes several seconds for his hand to form a fist and travel toward your head before it is intercepted by your move. Continue at this deliberate pace as he pushes the fist directly toward your face. Only the speed at which events occur should be changed; all the other elements of the movement must be kept realistic. This allows a more detailed understanding of the elements of the outside crane.

Do not make exaggerated motions; you won't be able to in a real fight because things happen too fast. Use the minimum force to displace the incoming strike; that is, just enough to make it miss when coordinated with your head movement. If done perfectly, virtually no force is used. Remember the concept of economy of movement.

Try this drill with your other hand (your left if you are right-handed) coming up to the outside of the opponent's elbow joint. Notice how this locks out the opponent's arm and forces it along a predetermined path and how you can combine this action with the slight draw down of his wrist to direct the path of the blow downward and toward you. (When I say "toward you," I mean that since the blow was going toward you in the first place and you have not radically changed its path, which would be contesting power, it is still coming toward you. It just does not hit you because you have slightly deflected the blow and moved your head out of the way.)

The blow's forward motion is not arrested as it would have been if it had hit your head solidly. Neither is it stopped as it would have been had you blocked it in the power style. Since that is the response your attacker is perceptually prepared for, and since you are drawing his blow in and down, the result often is that he is drawn greatly off balance. See how this works in the drill and realize that the more committed his strike, the greater his loss of balance can become.

Drill Two: The Boxer Blow

When you have practiced enough to have some control, have your training partner throw blows like a boxer would, snapping in and out very quickly. When the fist comes in and out this fast, there is little chance that it will overextend, which often means you will not be able to draw it down and destabilize your opponent as previously described. The boxer is a tougher cookie to deal with, so you must practice this drill seriously.

Note how the wrist need only slightly deflect the blow (when combined with your head movement) to render it harmless. Also, observe how your slipping hand can follow the fist back in slightly over the opponent's punching arm, allowing your counterstrike to land just as his shot is being pulled back. With perfect application, you will feel his returning hand help pull your shot into him.

Drill Three: Polishing the Return Strike

Execute the outside crane without the other hand going to the elbow. Note how you can still draw him down a little and be able to shoot that hand (vertical fist) over his striking arm into his nose. Do this very slowly at first. Observe that when the punch is thrown at you from an awkward facing (such as if you are not facing your attacker, he is off to the side, or maybe slightly behind you), you can still use this technique and return the vertical fist to the nose. The outside crane does not demand a full-facing position to work, though if you are turned away from your opponent, it is generally not possible to bring the other hand to his outside elbow.

Drill Four: Advanced Training at Full Speed

When practicing the outside crane on the straight punch, you should eventually get to the point where the training partner is throwing full-speed shots to your head. If you have head gear, use it. The opponent cannot wear any sort of glove that enlarges his hand or covers his wrist, however, so a boxing glove is no good. Light bag gloves are okay, though.

Obviously, full-speed training is dangerous. It should not be done until you have a very good feel for the move and have gradually increased speed during training.

It is no good if your partner is not aiming for your head, or if he is holding back and trying to avoid an accident by shooting the blow just off the mark. You will develop false gates this way. Make him throw the blow on the correct path and stop it before it lands.

When you have slipped his shot, you will see that you must make a slight, slipping advance into your man as you deliver the return strike. The return strikes that I have used most effectively from the outside crane are the vertical fist, the open hand to the throat, and, to a lesser extent, the palm heel to the face or chin.

Keeping a Realistic Perspective in These Training Drills
When you have practiced long enough and have made enough progress to begin full-speed drills, then you may notice two distinct phenomena. The first is that your form tends to break down. To go fast enough to prevent the blow from landing, you may get a little sloppy compared to the slow-motion drills. You may get the feeling that you are somehow leaving out parts of the movement. But if the guy is throwing the shot full force and full speed and it is not busting your head, then these parts you "left out" were not really needed. In fact, they were probably never part of the correct application of the technique in the first place.

In Chapter 2, I said real fights were sloppy affairs. When your training gets realistic enough to include full-speed, powerful attacks, it more closely simulates a real fight. The result: your execution begins to look a bit sloppy, too. Yet it is a real confidence builder when your training partner can throw spontaneous full-speed strikes to your head and not hit you.

There is no painful contact in these drills if they are done properly. In contrast, how many rising blocks can you practice against a full-speed shot before both individuals have some real painful arm bruises? What's more, the participants begin to flinch before they execute their movements as they anticipate the pain. This is very bad.

The second thing you may observe in full-speed training is that it seems peculiarly difficult for the opponent to hit you. You may actually begin to wonder how someone could be able to land a full-force shot on you once you have this move fairly well wired. Well again, I'm glad you asked.

There is a significant difference between training and an actual attack, even though the former may be full speed. In fact, your training partner's punch may actually be faster than your potential sucker puncher's strike, but there is still a big difference between the two. Primarily, in training you are perceptually ready for the exercise; a real attack is an ambush, a surprise attack. Yet if you are perceptually ready for an ambush, then you cannot be ambushed with total effectiveness. And how do we develop such a perceptual state of mind? *Awareness* and knowing your enemy's ways.

INSIDE CRANE DRILLS

Use the same line on the floor as in the outside crane exercises. As mentioned, the inside crane is used when you are inside your opponent's arms. Essentially you are facing each other straight on.

Drill One: Mechanics of the Inside Crane

First, you must understand the mechanics of this defense. The hook takes an arcing path toward your head. This arc gives the blow its power by providing a longer path for it to pick up speed. Also, body weight is shifted into the blow by raising the elbow just before impact. Like any punch, the better it is thrown, the harder it is to avoid. Boxers have good hooks, but anybody who might throw a haymaker is not a trained boxer.

However, the hook is a bit easier to defend against than the straight punch because you have a better chance of seeing it coming. More cues are offered during its preparation, and its arcing path provides motion in a near horizontal plane to your line of vision. Contrast this with a vertical fist rising up along a vertical plane to the victim's nose when the opponents are standing right next to each other. Pause a minute and really try to visualize this difference. It is a significant concept.

Also, the angle of attack is easier to determine with the hook, which means the position of the gate you must close to avoid getting hit is more apparent. Keep in mind, we are not trying to reach out and block the strike. We are not thinking in terms of seeing something coming and then trying to "catch" it. We only want to perceive the path it must come on. Then we make sure something is in the way along that path before the punch reaches its target.

Drill Two: Perceiving the Hook
and Finding Your Gates

Have your partner throw slow-motion hooks to your head while you watch the cues. The shoulder drop, head dropping below the angle of attack, and far shoulder pitching slightly forward are some basic cues for the hook. Discover the others for yourself during slow-motion drills and, later, during full-speed training.

Next, simply raise your hand on the same side of your body that the hook is coming in on. Place this hand at the proper gate. The position of your hand is at the attacker's wrist with the back of your wrist on his. Your hand is open and relaxed, and the fingers are naturally held in a somewhat upward position.

Return both of your hands to your side and have the hooks come in slowly once again, but this time use only the hand on the opposite side of your body to come across such that you place your palm on his arm near his wrist. This should intercept his incoming blow at the same gate position as before when you used the "same side" hand.

Now use both movements at the same time. If you are right-handed your right hand should be forward (closer to your opponent) and your left hand should be behind and touching your right hand at the wrist. This will displace your left hand off the attacker's wrist somewhat, but there still should be slight contact there. This is a variation of an X, or "iron fan," block.

Note how your hands support each other. If they are at the proper gate, then the punch has to blast through this entire assembly before it gets you. This will break any true focus it may have had. You still must drop your head out of the attack line that the punch would have followed had it not been intercepted at the gate.

Drill Three: Solo Practice for Speed and Gate Position

Without a training partner, practice throwing up your hands to close the gate to develop natural speed and coordination. They must move in a single motion. But you can only polish the technique and truly understand how it works when your partner throws near full-force hooks to your head. Of course, don't try this until you have practiced the move with this solo exercise and with a partner gradually increasing the speed of the hook.

In addition to the coordinated movement of the two hands coming up, make a slight step forward into your man, which will bring you inside his hook's effective power. This also puts you in position for the counterstrike.

Drill Four: Timing Lock-out and Relaxation

Concentrate on closing the gate before practicing the return strike. As contact is made with the incoming blow, there is a moment when your hands and arms "lock out" as the strike impacts. The instant the blow is defeated, your hands must relax for further dynamic motion.

In this exercise, your training partner throws moderate-speed hooks. You simply throw up your hands correctly and lock them out at the instant of impact. Then relax the hands and return them to your side without going through the rest of the movement. This will help you develop proper timing without the complication of adding the counterstrike. When this part of the technique is reasonably understood, then add the shuto, followed by the palm-heel to the solar plexus or the open-hand throat shot.

Drill Five: Using One Hand

Practice the head drop and the forward step using only the hand on the same side of your body that is being attacked. In a real fight against a real fast guy, this may be all you have time for.

Note that in this case, the single hand draws the blow along a forward path with just a slightly greater arc than otherwise would have been taken. Experiment with attempting to draw down the strike slightly as your hand turns out and over onto the opponent's arm, similar to the push down of the outside crane. On a poorly thrown blow, sometimes your hand will catch that bump where the opponent's wrist joins his hand. This occurs after the blow has spent its focus and can allow for a good draw down, which unbalances the less skillful attacker.

Realize that when using one hand for the inside crane, the movement of your head away from the hook becomes even more critical in avoiding the shot.

Drill Six: Return Strikes for the Inside Crane

When using both hands during the full technique, notice how your lead hand (right hand for right-handers and vice versa) is at high gate and perfectly positioned for the shuto to the opponent's neck. As you throw the shuto, withdraw your other hand in the opposite direction. Your two hands are moving away from each other to relax the nonstriking side of your body from static (stationary) resistance, which would rob power and speed from your shuto. This is a common concept for most blows.

Practice finding the natural flow of the palm heel to the solar plexus or floating ribs, which occurs when your shuto impacts and your hand comes back to chamber for the palm blow. The palm blow may be accompanied by a slightly further advance into the opponent to add power to the strike.

Eventually, put your strikes together in one continuous and flowing attack, imparting increasingly greater impact with each successive blow. Experiment with blows that flow from the palm-heel strike. The palm-heel uppercut is one; the open hand or elbow to the throat is another.

Keep in mind that you are striking with your entire body, not just a hand or elbow. This is accomplished by relaxation, which allows proper hip swing and thus a shift of body weight into the blows. When stepping into your man to deliver a strike, make sure the blow lands just before you transfer your weight to the lead foot. If it lands after the foot settles, it will not generate real power.

Drill Seven: Advanced Training; Going For It, Flat Out

Practice defending against both left and right hooks. Eventually, you should develop the inside crane to the point where your partner throws full-speed hooks to your head and you defeat them and flow into counterstrikes.

During training, it is not so necessary to flow into your return strikes with full speed. It can, in fact, be dangerous to practice. If you practice return strikes with moderate speed and proper form, work on your individual strikes with the toolbox drills, and go full contact on the heavy bag, you will be in good shape to strike a powerful blow when it's demanded against a real attacker. It is really a lot easier just to crack the hell out of somebody than it is to execute a blow with good form and power but pull the punch just before it lands.

The same cautions apply here as with the outside crane drills. Do it for form, then gradually work up speed. This allows you to get used to the distance so that your partner can throw a blow along its proper line and still pull the punch. Keep in mind that the proper attack line must be maintained as he throws the punch. Avoid a false attack angle that comes from a fear of accidentally hitting each other. But be careful; busted teeth don't grow back.

Once you think you have the crane defenses down pretty good and have done enough full-speed training with your partner pulling the punch, then you may want to try the next step. It is a bit dangerous, but basically have your training partner do his best to hit you for real.

Face each other, hands at your sides like the old western gunfight myth, and have him fire a spontaneous hook to your head with the intent to strike you. No holding back. If you can escape the blow, it will help you develop essential confidence in your ability to perform the technique, which will help you relax more in a real fight. It may actually help you avoid fights, too, when your "interviewer" perceives your confidence level.

Also, a full-speed shot that's pulled is different from one that would actually land. You will see the difference if you trained enough before you try this "go for it" drill. This way, that little difference won't slow you down in a real fight just because you are experiencing it for the first time.

Even if he does pop you in the head, you have almost certainly taken the best focus out of the shot. If you confine this advanced training to the hook, you should be able to avoid busting a jaw or losing some teeth. For training purposes, however, the punch should be thrown to the higher cheekbone, not to the teeth or orbital socket. But being hit has training value, too, because you tend to get used to it.

SOME OBSERVATION ABOUT PROPER COMBAT ATTITUDE

When I was working at the bar as a bouncer, I was also teaching at a karate school. I didn't let any of the students realize this, as most were too young to get into the bar anyway and we would have definitely carded them if they tried. (Actually, this unglamorous task is often a bouncer's primary activity.)

At the school, I would have students throw full-force, properly focused shots at me from the "gunfighter" position previously described. This allowed me to keep my reflexes up and gave me a good way to judge the students' progress and ability. It also gave me a means to see who needed more help with their combat attitude.

There are people who have difficulty actually hitting someone. I guess it's because of some cultural conditioning against violence. I must admit this is something of a mystery to me, but I know this attitude exists. Regardless of whether the circumstances call for violent action, some people will hesitate. This is disastrous. You must not trap yourself into this disabling mind-set. Since you cannot fix something until you know what is wrong, examine your own spirit for this problem. Don't discover it in a fight. It will be too late.

Sometimes I would discover this attitude from a student during this drill. There would be a slight turning away from the true attack line; something would be held back. While most of the students studied the art of karate, this was my self-defense class, not the karate class. They had paid me specifically to teach them to defend themselves in a real fight.

Consequently, I had an obligation to instill in them a functional combat attitude. Various strategies were used to cure people of any kind of thinking that prevented them from realizing and developing their own potential. All such strategies were conducted in private, away from the other students. I directed the attention of the student to the dangers—in fact, the totally disabling effects—of their attitude problem. Many times they could be made to recognize, understand, and ultimately overcome their problem through logic, training, and the enhancement of their self-image. Other times it was necessary to essentially force them to fight.

There was this one kid, a really decent person. He had most of the correct moves and all, but he lacked the proper combat attitude. I told him to wait after class so as not to embarrass him. I told him the objective of the lesson and had him throw his best shot, a hook, to my head. When I saw it was off line and not really intended to land with maximum power, I struck him with my open hand. He was absolutely stunned, not so much physically but psychologically. I had never really hit any students before, and I wasn't really hitting this guy. But for him, it was as real as it needed to be. I told him to throw the shot again. The result was similar, and so was my response.

As he got up, I made remarks concerning both his racial heritage and the circumstances of his birth and hit him again as he was getting to his feet. I then stuck my chin out in an exaggerated manner, taunting him to swing on me as I continued with some pretty imaginative verbal abuse. I saw his shot coming and it landed pretty good. He was pissed and I fell to the mat for him. It made me feel great, like some sort of liberator.

I got up like nothing had happened and resumed my normal classroom demeanor and tone of speech with which he was familiar. "Very good," I said. "Next we work on more power. Then you must learn to deliver the blow with effectiveness but with a clear mind. An angry mind is seldom a clear one." I had this speech prepared for some time. You see, I knew I could get his mind right; he was the one who needed to discover it. Besides, if I was going to take a shot from a student for his own benefit, I figured I had at least earned the right to play "mystic master" for a minute. My jaw was actually a little stiff for several days. This showed he had some focus because I rolled with the shot to prevent any real injury to myself.

The point? Even if you learn all the strikes and simple throws, how to slip a blow, and everything else, you will not prevail in an actual attack without proper combat attitude. At the most elementary level, this means some measure of mental control (relaxation) during combat while you invest your strikes or flight strategy with an expansive emotional content.

"So what the hell is he saying?," you may well ask.

Okay, here it is another way. If you are afraid to hurt someone, to whatever degree and for whatever misguided reason, then you will hesitate to that same degree when the time comes for the real thing. This hesitation can be all your enemy needs to overcome you.

On the other hand, if you are in a complete rage, a full-on blood lust to kill, then not only might you be on your way to a long prison term, but you actually won't be fighting as well as you could otherwise because you are not in control of yourself.

True, blood lust is a better combat attitude than hesitation or fear, but it is not always the most combat-effective attitude because it prevents proper thinking. This is okay in some rare life-or-death situations, especially if you're fighting against weapons. But anytime you shut down your brain, you are putting on hold your very best weapon. The brain allows or precludes the use of all other tools.

There is another important aspect of combat attitude that relates quite directly to your formation of that "I'm not going to prison" plan. You remember, the one we talked about in the first few pages of this book? Golly, wonder why I put it there?

CREATING OPTIONS FOR YOURSELF BETWEEN NORMAL AND COMBAT-KILL MODES

If you have the right combat attitude, you don't allow someone to get you into a totally berserk "blast their fucking brains into a fucking pink mist" attitude. You must have more choices than what I call "normal" and "combat-kill" modes.

Curiously, the person afraid to hurt someone who does not explore this problem not only risks his enemy closing his medical record, but also risks going into combat-kill mode for the first time in his life when it may not be demanded for his survival.

Here is such an example. A guy freaks when somebody punches him out a bit. He thinks he's going to die, so he picks a fire extinguisher off the wall and bashes the guy's brains out by whacking him in the head a dozen times in a panicked frenzy. The presence of firearms and knives make this escalation of the conflict real easy. You might say, "So what? The guy was attacked. It's self-defense."

If this is your attitude, pal, then you have a good chance of writing your own book; something like *Inside Folsom Prison*, or maybe *The Hate Factory*. The second title is a real book by a prisoner in New Mexico. You might need to find a copy and read it; it may help motivate your "I'm not going to prison" plan. You might also benefit by a little elementary study of the law. You can get this opportunity in prison, too. Every prison has a law library. Can you guess why?

Sometimes when somebody really does something to piss me off, but it isn't really necessary from a personal defense standpoint to bust his head, I still may feel that old "spill the wine" protorage building up in me gutty wuts. But I try some alternative strategy to pounding him. I do not ignore him because that would either encourage an ambush or, at the least, leave me with unresolved hostility. I might just look him right in the eye and smile "pleasantly," which can get pretty scary.

The point is, I give myself somewhere else to go mentally besides combat-kill mode. Most often, if a person is testing me out with a remark or interview of some sort, I can just stop the whole proceedings right off the bat with a word or a look, as described in previous chapters. Not only can this defuse the ambush, it also helps prevent me from being pushed, incrementally, into combat mode. Besides, if I let someone get me boiling mad, he may well be more in control of me than I am of myself.

Figure out some alternatives for yourself and

recognize why you need them. I am speaking mostly to the reader who has experienced the rage that can lead to physical conflicts with all their potentially disastrous consequences as well as unnecessary legal problems. Learn to control yourself and your instinct to kill or it may one day destroy you.

Now for the people who have the "other" problem—difficulty employing effective violence in their self-defense. Since I have never experienced hesitation to do violence when it was needed, I can not speak from experience here. I will stick my neck out and try to generalize from other personal experiences and observations.

The first step is to try to figure out why you feel this way. Dealing with some of my unwanted attitudes that I have partially purged myself of or at least have controlled better always really began with an honest look inward. Why I did what I did; why I really felt as I felt.

If I felt I might have trouble, psychologically speaking, performing some action in the future, I would try to mentally visualize myself performing that activity correctly. I would run this movie in my mind's eye all the time until performance time came.

When I was much younger, I would do this to prepare myself for a big karate tournament. Bringing to my mind's eye a picture of my chief opponent, I would imagine him falling to the mat after my perfect sweep or some such technique. Later, I used this visualization technique for my first few parachute jumps.

It may be that if you cannot truly visualize yourself doing something like defending yourself, then you are not psychologically prepared for that activity in reality. At the very least you might use this visualization concept to "test" your mental preparedness to engage your enemy and do the damage demanded to defeat him.

From another point of view, consider the nature of the bully. If he is allowed to abuse others mentally and physically, he is only further encouraged to continue. Therefore, if you do not resist him, do you not share some degree of responsibility for the injury he does to others as well as yourself? Perhaps his next victim will be even less prepared than yourself to deal with such aggression effectively. Consider this: if everyone, everywhere, immediately resisted to their fullest all forms of tyranny, where would the bullies go? How would the Nazis have ever have gotten started?

The true spirit of the warrior is found in the desire to defend the weaker against the aggression of the stronger. In this way an essential balance is kept in the world. The warrior trains so that he will be prepared and will thus not fail in his role.

CHAPTER 5

MOBILITY, STANCE, FACING, AND THE FINER POINTS OF STAYING OUT OF JAIL

Classical martial arts make much of stance—the horse stance, on-guard position, and so forth. The thing to realize here is that when you're attacked, your "stance" will be (at least initially) no more than how you happen to be standing at the moment of attack. The ambusher chooses the moment of attack, and you can be sure he will make his move when he feels your stance and facing position are weakest.

Any fight where your opponent gives you the chance to square off with him, as in raising his hands in challenge and calling out to you, "Cum on mudda fucker!" is not really a fight in my book. It certainly isn't an ambush. It is more of a heated athletic contest. You can be hurt pretty good in such contests, and they are certainly to be avoided. But the point is that most of the time this type of challenge can simply be declined, thus it is generally rather easy to avoid.

In reality, the guy may be boiling mad at you for one reason or another, but his calling out the challenge, in most cases, is partly to give you a chance to decline. It may not seem this way to look at the guy with his veins sticking out on his neck and all that. But think about it. If his only objective were to punch your lights out, he would have gone directly to it with an ambush. Some part of him is looking for another way. He may even have some foggy notion of making it a "fair" contest.

In my world, a real fight simply is not any sort of a contest, fair or otherwise.

Consider this obvious fact about the guy challenging you to fight. He's challenging, not attacking. This means that something is holding him back. It may be because of some realization that if he gets into a fight, he could face legal problems. His challenge may be something of an attempt to make it alright legally, especially if you take up the challenge for all to see. This is the thought process in the cretin's "mind" on a near subconscious level.

Also keep in mind that a challenge to fight can be seen as the final stage of a very hot interview. Think what that means.

The bottom line is, if you decline, then he may be satisfied since everybody will see this, too. He gets to feel macho. Of course, he may still go into some woofing as you leave the establishment or other location. This often takes the form of, "You yellow-bellied sack of shit! Come back here!" etc., etc. But does he really want you to come back? In my experience, he usually does not despite his verbal berating as you leave.

This loud mouth's bellowing should not bother you in the least *if* you are in control of yourself. Be attentive to his tone and choice of words, however, because every now and then the additional verbal abuse will encourage the guy to close the distance and attack. If so, this will most probably be in the form of a quick ambush on your back as you turn to leave. Be alert!

Be prepared to go into a flight and reverse ambush or something even simpler. Again, he cannot really ambush you now because you are alert. You should say something like, "Get away from me, man. I don't want any part of this bullshit!" Do this as soon as he makes his first verbal challenge to fight.

Consider using the term "machismo bullshit." I have observed that later on, should the local police take statements after placing you in handcuffs, women seem to remember this particular remark. This makes them better witnesses for you. The point is to create for yourself, before any violence, potential witnesses whose statements will support your self-defense claim. This way if he closes for the ambush and you whip around with a pool cue, pitcher of beer, or chair to his fucking head, it will be better for your legal defense later.

You may need to express your concern to the assembled multitude that you are aware that your challenger is armed. Consider beforehand that things could get real sticky if, for instance, your swinging chair trick breaks the fucker's neck. It will help you out a lot if somebody testifies, "Well, I heard him yell out to the guy, 'Get away from me. I don't want to fight. I know you got that knife!' Then when the guy rushed on him, he swung that chair."

Generally, if it comes to a fight, you are going to spend at least that particular night in the local jail. There can be exceptions, though, depending on how well you have set up things for that effective testimony before the shit hit the fan. Of course, it's better just to leave before the shit hits the fan.

There have been incidents where I had to blast somebody after his woofing went to ambush as I was departing. On two such occasions, the collective statements of everybody the cops interviewed at the scene made it so clear that there was no case for an assault charge that I didn't even have to go to jail that night. Naturally, they ran me through the NCC (National Crime Computer) for warrants before cutting me loose. But I didn't have to worry about that because of the effectiveness of my "I'm not going to prison" plan. You see, I don't have any warrants on my ass.

If you stay in control of yourself and don't let somebody control you simply with words, then you will be clearheaded enough to think about setting up testimony potential from jump street. You will also be thinking straight enough to realize that you are in a no-win situation when challenged to fight, and that leaving the scene is the best thing for that very special person in your life—namely, you.

THE OBJECTIVES OF PROPER STANCE

Stance and mobility must be considered as two sides of the same coin. Mobility, which is the capacity to move your body quickly, is always somewhat at odds with stability. If your stance is not stable (that is, well balanced), you are easily knocked down. On the other hand, if your stance is too rooted with an extremely low center of gravity, it would be very stable but it would be rather slow to make the transition to mobility.

The classic horse stance of most Asian systems can be quite strong on stability (at least in one direction) but it is rather immobile. Its use in real fighting is rather limited, but it is still important to know. An example would be after your opponent is so damaged that he is incapable of counterattack (read *semiconscious*). In this case you might fall into a horse stance to better ground your next punch for extra power. Another use for the horse stance would be during grappling and escapes to help keep you from being knocked off your feet before you can start to move and counter.

Keep in mind the characteristics of real fights that I listed in Chapter 2: they begin with some form of ambush, most end in some form of grappling, punches to the head are most often the decisive blows, and they're over in a matter of seconds. In contrast, the elements of a martial arts sparring session are quite different. The attention now is on the tactical use of stance, distance, and mobility.

When I would be free sparring in a karate match, there was a lot of emphasis on reading the opponent's fight strategy, discovering his preferred techniques, setting up feints, and chaining combinations of techniques for compound attacks. This meant constantly changing one's facing accompanied by slight adjustments in distance in an effort to create or discover an opening. I never "danced" about my opponent like some dojo ballerinas, but you can't just stand there against the trained fighter, not even in an athletic contest of this sort.

In a real street or bar fight, such movements and tactics rarely come into play because everybody is just going for it. They aren't playing at fighting; they're trying to put the other guy away. They are much less controlled than persons involved in a tactical sparring match. Contrast this situation with sport free sparring where no one is emotionally involved and nobody is supposed to get hurt.

If you study a martial art, it is essential that you realize this difference between a sparring contest and a real fight. Many of the clever feints, compound attacks, and methods of making your opponent throw a given technique that may be decisive in a karate contest simply do not apply to a real fight. When practicing in a dojo, learn to discriminate between these two situations. Ask yourself if it is you that is simply a "point" fighter.

There are karateka who can out-point me every time in the dojo, but who would not last more than a few seconds against me in a real fight. There are also karateka that can out-point me in the dojo and also break my bones in a real fight.

Free sparring is a worthwhile training method because it does give some dynamics to training and it can improve your perception of the blow, the critical concept of distance, as well as your general reflexes. You must, however, not cloud your mind in an actual fight with a "wait and see what he's doing" strategy as in your free-sparring practice. You have to "go for it" too. This does not mean you hurl yourself at your opponent in an overextended or overcommitted manner. This is where the concepts of mobility, balance, facing, and stability come into play for real.

FACING FORWARD WITH YOUR STRONG SIDE

It is an axiom in Western boxing that, assuming you are a right-handed person, you never lead with your right hand because it is the power hand. An opening must first be created with the left before the power hand has a decent chance to land. Leading with the right also exposes you to the counterpunch since the right lead tends to be an overextended blow. The boxer engages his opponent's defense with the left jab to get him in motion and thus create an opening for the right power hand to land.

However, all this refers to a boxing match, not a real fight. These boxing tactics are not so different from the karate match I talked about earlier. The tactics and axioms of these sports do not always apply well to a real fight. As I've already mentioned, though, boxing, because of its contact training method and its exclusive use of hand combinations as the tools, is generally more applicable to real fighting than are most martial arts. In fact, most boxers are mentally tougher than most martial artists because of the contact training methods.

If you are right-handed, then your right hand is probably much more coordinated and stronger than your left hand. To demonstrate this to yourself, try to write with your left hand or do any of a number of activities you normally do with your right. You will discover that your "weak" hand is surprisingly clumsy.

A left-handed person is different because we live in a basically right-handed culture. This means the left-hander learns to use both hands with more dexterity than a right-hander. In effect, he has two "right hands." This makes the left-handed fighter a bit difficult to deal with. Some left-handed professional boxers of only ordinary ability will rise higher in their careers simply because of this natural advantage.

If your potential opponent gives you a chance, such as just before or during an interview, one of the first things you want to observe is whether he is right- or left-handed. This will give you an extra split second to anticipate his punch.

Now to the primary point of all this. If you are right-handed, you are also very likely to be right-legged. You should face your opponent with your right leg forward and your right hand closest to him. This is what is meant by having your strong side forward. This puts your stronger and more coordinated limb up front, ready to apply the crane defenses that we looked at earlier. If you are left-handed the situation is simply reversed, but you will have to experiment to find out if this is indeed the case for you.

Keep in mind that real fights don't involve much, if any, dancing, feints, or compound attacks. You will only have a split second to turn toward your attacker when he launches his ambush. If possible, you want your best hand forward to break the focus of his incoming blow.

With practice, you can actually slip the blow with your right and then "pass" the attacker's limb to your left for momentary retention while your right flows directly into a chambering for the counterpunch. This is the essence of a well-executed crane defense. It is not exactly leading with your right hand because it has slipped the opponent's blow first. The left is used to keep the opening open, setting up the blow from your right hand.

The second aspect of facing with your strong side

forward is that your strong leg is closest to your opponent. This makes it easier for you to push off for the slipping-back retreat we will look at shortly. The forward advance is also aided by having your stronger and more coordinated leg up front.

CONTROLLING DISTANCE: THE ADVANTAGE OF CLOSING ON YOUR ATTACKER

In your heavy-bag training, you will discover how close you have to be to land a good solid punch. The distance is closer than many martial arts students realize because they don't do much full-contact training. You really have to be quite close to use the open hand to the throat or the palm-heel strike to the solar plexus or floating ribs. The vertical fist and backfist can be used a bit farther out.

Regardless of the blow, you have to have the willingness and ability to close on your opponent in order to land an effective strike. This is an important aspect of controlling distance.

Personally, I like being close to my attacker after slipping his blow because it has worked for me so many times. When a guy swung on me and I closed distance so that I was right up next to him, almost chest to chest, he didn't like it at all. The guy would try to open the distance not only because he was uncomfortable with me that close, but also because he couldn't land a good punch at that distance. While he was moving back, he couldn't land a solid shot either, as most fighters can't land a good punch when they are moving back. Muhammad Ali could, but he may have been the greatest fighter who ever lived, and that's a far cry from your typical saloon warrior.

The result? I would control the distance of the fight because my opponent was a one-distance fighter. He would try to get back to the distance where he felt he could work. Needless to say, I would never give him a chance to do that.

In order to close distance on a man quick enough to avoid being hit on the way in, you must develop a few key attributes. These attributes are: a) proper timing, which depends on an accurate perception of the opponent's blow; b) the ability to make a quick, shuffling advance, which we will describe shortly; and c) the psychological willingness to close with the enemy. The first two attributes are of no value if you don't have the third. This must come from training if not from actual fight experience.

When I think back on some of the battles I have been in, it occurs to me that I really wasn't so damn fast or powerful, nor was my technique very clean or tricky. Many times, the decisive factor was that I moved right into the guy. There was no hesitation—it was an instantaneous counterattack at a distance my opponent was unprepared to deal with.

Not every situation will call for instantly closing with the attacker. However, in almost every surprise attack from a saloon warrior that I have been the subject of, this is exactly what I did. Even when my tactical judgment told me that escape was the best strategy, I would still close first.

The worst thing you can do is halfheartedly close on the guy. You need to be right up on him, where your chests might be four or five inches apart and maybe touching for a moment. Moreover, you have to be there instantly.

I think I really tumbled into this after the first few times I was attacked with pool cues and, later, a tire iron. I knew that these weapons were real dangerous when I was within their range, a bit longer than normal arm's length. Not wanting to get hit out there, I rushed in and jammed the attack. If the initial distance had been a little greater, then I could have safely opened it up even more and interposed a table, car, or other object between us, or picked up my own improvised weapon. As it was, if I had opened up the distance during these attacks, I would very likely have been hit at the ideal range of the weapon. By closing, I got inside its effective range.

Weapon attacks accentuate the importance of the concept of controlling distance to get inside or outside the effective range of a blow. When most people pick up a weapon and attack you with it, they often put all of their confidence and strategy in the weapon alone (knives are different if in the hands of an experienced knifer). Defeat the weapon and you defeat them, and you therefore defeat the attack.

Another tactical concept in dealing with a weapon like a stick is that the assailant expects you to move away from his weapon. He tries to close on you and use the superior range of his tool. He is not at all well prepared, psychologically or gate and timing wise, for you to instantly close the distance on him.

I use the example of a weapon attack because I think the greater range of a weapon makes this principle of controlling distance easier to grasp. The Filipino martial arts, including escrima, kali, and arnis, have a keen appreciation of this fact. The concept of tactical movement and distance is actually the same whether the attacker has a stick or is only using his empty hand. The following is an example of this concept as it applies to the stick. This incident occurred early in my career as a bouncer.

I had told this guy earlier in the evening to stop harassing a patron he was verbally fucking with or he would have to leave. A bit later I heard his loud, obnoxious mouth again. Very bad for business, so I went over to escort him out.

Next thing I see, he has a pool cue in his hand and is closing on me real fast, swinging it at my head from high gate. I just sped up my pace with a quick, shuffling slide and closed the distance between us. My left hand went to his shoulder and checked his blow as my head moved out of the attack line and into him. I did not put my head down such that I could not see—my eyes remained on him. This is an important aspect of evasive head movement to remember.

Because I was a little excited, I forgot myself and punched him in the face with a powerful overhead right, a closed-fist blow. I was pissed. Disarming him of the pool cue, I began choking him from behind with it while I shouted something like, "You wanna hit me with this, asshole?! You wanna hit me with this?!" Each time I said this I jerked the stick into his throat.

This was very uncool on my part, very un-professional, but I was new to the business at that time and didn't know how to act. I was still taking shit personally. In a second the other bouncers were there cooling me down.

The guy was eighty-sixed permanently. I got the deserved and helpful lecture from a more experienced doorman on why not to do this shit. It made me feel like a little kid. The head doorman sent me home for the night (with pay), even though it was early in the evening. I guess he knew I was pumped up and therefore a potential liability to the establishment.

Because I had lost control and hit the guy in the head with my closed fist, my hand swelled so bad I could not comfortably shake hands with anybody for a week or so. Luckily, I broke no bones.

One of the lessons that stuck with me regarding this incident was that the guy could have done a lot of things to keep me from getting him like that, only he didn't. I thought, "Shit! If I had that pool cue I would have made it work." The difference was that he was psychologically defeated when his weapon failed at the moment I jammed his strike. He was unable to make the mental shift into a defense or counterattack without the weapon.

A large part of his inability to shift into an effective

defense or counterattack was because of his failure to immediately change his fighting distance. This is a significant point because to an extent the average sucker puncher sometimes succumbs to this same problem, which results from being a one-strategy and/or one-distance fighter. When you defeat the opening sucker punch, his one strategy has failed. This is a big reason why closing the distance with an immediate and continuous counterattack after slipping the blow can work for you so well.

The truth is, the guy who attacked me with the pool cue had backed up a half step, and there was a slight delay before my haymaker connected. He actually had time to block it with his free hand but failed to do so. Without the pool cue, I think he might have blocked it. It wouldn't have been any great feat to get something in the way, but he didn't even move his head. In defeating his weapon, I had defeated him, and this was tactically accomplished by my controlling the distance during the incident.

THE EIGHT ANGLES OF MOVEMENT

We are going to talk about techniques like the sliding-up advance, the sidestep to a corner, and the controlled slipping-back retreat. However, before we think about how to move, let's look at where you are moving to and from where your attacker moves on you.

Picture a circle divided into eight equal parts. You could divide the circle up into sixteen, twenty, and so on, but given the average size of the human body and the basic distance from which one person is able to deliver a strike to another, eight directions is as fine as you need to cut it.

We will call the four basic directions (right, left, forward, and back) the primaries. The other four angles, the corners, lie between each of the primaries. Most times the sucker puncher will attack from one of the corners. Conversely, when someone is attacking you from a primary angle, you want to slide off to a corner to some degree. Try to visualize this; later you will practice it in the drills.

Moving to a corner is a form of sidestepping an attack. Keep in mind, when someone is charging you, it is not so much the charge you are sidestepping but some particular blow or grab. To truly understand this, you need to practice the drills. For the moment, imagine a guy is charging in real fast and very aggressively. You must instantly spot the "true" attack. Are his hands held high or low? Do they hold a weapon?

If the hands are at midgate and slightly reaching out for you in advance of the guy's body (no chambering of a blow), this could be a variation of what I call the "Rhino." I got this term from a Canadian bouncer, Mr. W. Hay, who wrote me after studying one of my instructional videos.

The description he gave was a classic saloon-warrior move. In essence, the Rhino is when a guy charges into another person and throws him to the ground in order to stomp and kick him. It may include a punch on the way in, but that would really be an attempt to buy the attacker cover as he closed on his opponent. It is also meant to give the attacker a good chance to catch the guy's arms in preparation for the throw.

The Rhino throw is no more than a quick twisting of the victim's body above his center of gravity accompanied by the attacker's body weight slamming into the guy. Some Rhinos are more polished than others, but this is the general concept.

Sounds crude as hell, huh? It is. As I said earlier, real fights are generally crude and sloppy affairs.

But guess what? In the fights that I have seen it used in, the Rhino often works very well. Despite this, it is not to difficult to defend against if you are alert and have a good perception of angle of attack and distance. The mistake most people make is psychological. They perceive that the guy is coming in to knock them down, so they nearly instinctually "root" their bodies into the ground with a strong stance in an attempt to keep their balance against the attack.

Of course you won't make this mistake because, having read this book carefully and done the drills, you will know that such a strategy is based on contesting the opponent's power and that this is not the True Way. Instead, you will gracefully sidestep the Rhino at the last moment by sliding off to one corner. Then you will control the guy's momentum just enough to redirect it. Such redirection could be towards the floor, into a post, against an automobile . . . (We've been here before, haven't we?)

Once again, in the Rhino we see a one-strategy attack. You must learn to identify the nature of the assault at once and avoid it just like you perceived the straight punch or hook and were able to respond appropriately. This will always mean to not contest the power of the assault directly but avoid it and allow the opponent's forward motion to continue while you redirect it.

Notice how this is *conceptually* the exact same thing as the inside or outside crane, when the attack was a punch. With the Rhino, the attack is the guy's whole body rushing upon you, but the concepts are identical to avoiding a hook or straight punch. We will look at the details in the drills, but what I want you to appreciate here is what I meant when I remarked earlier that, with enough experience, CONCEPTS are more important than TECHNIQUES.

THE ERROR IN ACTION/REACTION THINKING

The mark of an experienced and capable martial artist who is also a good fighter is the ability to generalize everything that he has ever learned, instantly and fluidly, to the particular assault at hand. This means concepts are more important than technique.

It is a basic mistake to think or train exclusively in terms of a "he does this so I do that" mentality. This will seldom work in a real fight. It may actually lock your mind in an anxiety over, "What is he doing? What am I supposed to do?" Mind controls body, so you will be paralyzed in an evaluation/decision loop.

If you can think of all the tactics I put forth in this book in terms of concept and flow, you will have a more functional mind-set. This means you will perceive a hook and your body instantly moves in where it is safe while your hands automatically are thrown up in the way. When you feel that slap of his hands on yours, you counterstrike and continue with the counterattack. It is surprising how you can develop this if you train enough and have the right attitude.

In some fights I have been in, I had no clear recognition of the exact technique I used to put the attacker down. Blows are easier to remember because you feel the impact when they land and sometimes your hands hurt afterwards. But, as many fights end in grappling, I have often used some kind of throw to terminate the assault. In these cases I often couldn't really remember what I did to make the guy fall. In a sense, you sometimes have to make up a technique on the spot. This is what is meant by concept being more important than technique.

There are so many ways a person can grab onto you, and people vary so much in their reach, height, speed and so forth, that a prearranged technique or sequence that works on your training partner might fail on a person with a different body type or if the attack comes just a little differently. You need to get to the point where your mind flows with concepts rather than selects techniques when attacked. This is difficult and requires lengthy training as well as some actual experience. But this is the True Way.

Some martial arts, such as aikido, are predominantly

conceptually rather than technique oriented. I think one needs a balance here, but too often many martial artists tend to rely too heavily on technique.

I identify this rather advanced state of combat experience now because it will help you get a grasp of the ultimate goal of your training. It will give you some idea of how to gauge progress and hopefully prevent "robotic" thinking, which means robotic movement. Fighting is dynamic; it is alive, it flows. So must you to prevail.

A basic example of a general concept is to push when you are pulled, pull when you are pushed. This is simply another side of not contesting your opponent's power. If you make such a concept part of your mind and body, your body will always move correctly and even unexpectedly for your enemy. This is ironic, since so often what appears to be the natural reaction is not the best tactical survival response.

Moving forward, backward, or to the sides, it is the same thing. There is no time for thought. Train hard and you will be able to simply perceive and move.

OBJECTIVES OF THE SLIDING-UP ADVANCE AND SLIPPING-BACK RETREAT

The sliding-up advance is used primarily to step into your opponent in order to bring your tools into the ideal range. It is also used to jam an opponent's tools by moving inside their effective range.

When your advance is fast and fluid enough, then you miss being hit entirely on the way in. If you are a little late on the perception of the attack or in the execution of the advance, you may catch a piece of the blow, but not its full power. This way you are still able to launch a counterattack.

The slipping-back retreat is used to open the distance between an opponent so that you are away from the limit of his blow. When you practice with the heavy bag, candles, and cloth, you will better appreciate the fact that a blow only has real knockout power at a limited range of distance. If the target is a little too close or too far away, the point of focus is missed. When you step back, you put the target a little too far away. When you step in, you put the target a little too close. In either case, you will not always be able to avoid the blow entirely under actual fight circumstances, but you should be able to spoil its focus and thus avoid being "put away."

With the slipping-back retreat, you want to move back no further than is demanded for the blow to fail. This way, you are still close enough to step back in and counterattack. Further, if you retreat too far back, your opponent can continue his advance. This can result in a sequence that drives you under his control, as once you are forced to make three quick steps back along the same line, it can be difficult to sidestep.

THE SLIDING-UP ADVANCE

When you are facing with your strong side forward, your right hand and leg are forward (assuming you are right-handed). Most of your weight is on the rear leg so the forward leg can have greater mobility. A few would-be Bruce Lees out there have been taught to kick at the lead knee to disable an opponent. Such a kick is most damaging only when nearly your full body weight lands on the leg being attacked. While this knee attack is greatly overrated (like groin kicks), you do want to avoid giving this shot away to an opponent who may have a well-focused kick, so be wary of it.

To advance forward from this stance, push off with the rear leg as you raise the forward foot just high enough to clear the floor. Your front foot slips up to determine the length of the advance. When the front foot sets down, the rear foot has caught up and you arrive at the advanced position in exactly the same stance as you started. The advance is made along a direct line to your intended position on the opponent. This is the shortest distance. There is no wasted motion in this simple move.

The shoulders do not dip or turn much with this advance. The upper body is held in dynamic stability. This helps avoid telegraphing your blow to your opponent. Keep in mind that the sucker puncher knows most of the cues that foreshadow a blow. You want to deny him these cues so your blow will land.

However, never take up an overly rigid posture when trying to prevent telegraphing. Permit the shoulder to pitch slightly forward when you strike. This is a real no-no in classic karate, especially in taekwon-do. But it's the way to go in a real fight. Again, your heavy bag practice will demonstrate that you get more power this way.

You must learn how to properly execute the sliding-up advance, as it is a foundation concept. Your legs and footwork are what bring your tools into striking distance. Without a decent advance, you may never get a chance to use your tools on your opponent. On the other hand, I have used this simple advance combined with a rising vertical fist to whack opponents in the nose in such a way that they seemed to stand there offering no defense at all. This is because the average saloon warrior is not familiar with this advance. When you close on him real fast and fluid, he is confused for an instant. An instant is all he's got since he is not too familiar with a vertical fist either, and he hasn't seen any shoulder movement to react to. His mind may stop for a split second. The next thing he sees is purple dots against a black background.

Do not lean forward or back in your advance. Keep your feet almost directly beneath your shoulders. The advance is made in a manner that keeps you balanced at all times. The push off is done from the ball of the rear foot. Your lead foot arrives on the ball as well. Do not raise yourself up high on your toes like some fancy boxer. Bend the knees slightly to lower your center of gravity as you travel.

There is no real objective served in my beating this thing to death. The sliding-up advance is really very simple. I have given you the mechanics of it. The drills will help you integrate your tools with the advance. You will know when you have done this advance correctly; it will just feel right. It is real quick but controlled; you maintain balance through the entire movement and are never overextended. The most common mistake is to try to cover too much ground in a single advance. Avoid leaning forward!

Test your advance with the heavy bag. Stand away from the bag such that you must advance before you get in range for a well-focused strike. Then move up quickly and coordinate the landing of your blow with the settling of your weight forward so that the blow carries your full body weight at the instant it lands. After the blow lands, you should be back in your original stance with the forward leg supporting only a portion of your body weight, in good balance, and prepared to either advance further or retreat immediately.

THE SLIPPING-BACK RETREAT

Here we have another fundamental move that must be placed into your inventory of fighting skills. The slipping-back retreat is basically the reverse of the advance.

The front foot pushes back while the rear foot raises up just enough to clear the floor. You arrive at the rearward position in exactly the same stance as when you began the movement. The slight bending of the knee, traveling on the ball of the foot, and so on are all the same as in the advance.

Do not lean backward or forward with your

shoulders. The exception is when you must duck or whip your head back to avoid a blow to the head.

The secret of using the slipping-back retreat effectively in a fight is to have a good judgment of distance. This allows you to move back just far enough to make the blow miss or otherwise fail. In this way you are right there for the counterpunch. The easiest time to land a blow is just after your opponent has expended his shot. If you move back too far, then you have to close the distance again and therefore cannot deliver a counterpunch immediately.

Another problem with moving back too far is that it encourages your opponent to drive forward, forcing you to step back again. Most people cannot execute more than two or three quick, consecutive slipping-back retreats without losing some balance. Also, it is difficult to break away with the sidestep when being driven back like this.

Stepping or leaning back too far are the most common mistakes with this technique. Against a fast and well-executed ambush it may be demanded, but you must recover balance at once as the attacker's hand is pulled back from his blow. Of course a person who has mastered this will never lean back because his perception of the blow will be such that he is never caught that much by surprise.

MOVEMENT AND FACING DRILLS

Draw a circle on the ground approximately equal in diameter to your height or the length from fingertip to fingertip when you hold your arms straight out to your sides. For most people, these two measures are about the same.

Divide the circle into four equal parts with marks on the circumference. Subdivide the space equally between each of these marks so that you now have a circle divided into eight equal pieces.

This next drill may seem hopelessly simple. Do it anyway.

With your strong side facing one of the primaries, have your partner move to each of the eight positions on the circle and assume an attack stance. He does not enter the circle. Have him move to each position again, but this time a few steps outside the edge of the perimeter.

At first, do not turn to face him. Observe when he comes into your field of view from each position and how much you can see of his body without moving your eyes. Of course you will be unable to see him when he's directly behind you and probably when he's at the two rearward corners as well. Try this and find out.

Next, your partner stands directly in front of you while you take a strong-side facing on him. As he moves to each station, match his movement to keep the same facing on him. If you have more than one training partner, have them move to any of the stations on the circle while you change facing on both of them. The objective of this is to get you used to shifting to a new facing position instinctually and instantly with a simple, fluid motion that has no wasted movement and is executed in a casual and relaxed manner.

When approached for an interview, you want to move to strong-side facing without any great show. Nonetheless, the potential ambusher will note your subtle movement into this position and will know that you may be a bit too alert for an ideal ambush prospect.

All this may seem simple and of questionable value to you, but don't let this prevent you from doing this drill from time to time. If you never do it you will have made a serious error.

Slipping-Back Retreat Drill

Using the same circle from the previous drill, have your partner move into the circle from one of the stations while you change facing and slide back to the appropriate corner. Do not slip away further than the perimeter of the circle. Your partner enters into the circle with a sliding-up advance but only to the center, and only with one advance. He does not pursue you further. Remember, this is simply a perception drill.

Learn how you must turn and move with minimum motions and efforts to achieve strong-side facing. This is done at a walking pace or slower at first. When you discover how you must turn and move and are comfortable with the form of the slipping-back retreat and particularly with its economy of movement, only then should you pick up the pace of your partner's advance.

Ultimately, your partner will make the advance as fast as he can. This will sometimes result in body contact when he comes from a rearward facing. Discover how you must move to maintain balance while turning for proper facing and when body contact occurs while you continue the retreat.

Finding-the-Distance Drill

Have your partner stand still while you move up to the ideal distance for a palm heel to the solar plexus, vertical fist to the nose, open hand to the throat shot, or other strike. Keep in mind that the human body gives a little more on impact than the heavy bag, and you are trying to blast *through* the opponent rather than hit him on the surface of the target area.

Before doing the drill, it helps to actually feel the target area on your partner with the impact area of the strike you've chosen. For example, feel how the ribs move while your partner holds his body in one place.

In getting the vertical fist and backfist distance, extend the blow in slow motion but with proper form so that it touches the target area. Note your foot position in relation to your training partner. Observe the distance between your chest and his with these two blows. Also note how vulnerable your leg position makes you to a knee to your groin in relation to his facing.

The palm-heel strike, reverse punch, and throat shot are thrown from a closer distance than a vertical fist or backfist. However, this difference is not so great as one might think without having done this exercise. The fact is, all the striking tools that I have put forth here are close-in weapons. Like I said, I like to fight my opponent close in because it helps me control distance on him better.

When you have determined the distance from which you can best land a powerful blow with each of the strikes, proceed with the drill itself.

Marker Drills for Advancing and Retreating

Place a piece of tape on the floor to represent the opponent's position. Place a second piece of tape slightly in front of the first piece at a distance from which you would execute a given blow at the opponent. Without looking down at the tape, learn to make a quick sliding-up advance so that your lead foot arrives on or very near the second piece of tape.

Place a third piece of tape at a distance from which the opponent could not quite reach you with a hook or straight punch. Practice a quick slipping-back retreat from the position where you could deliver a blow to the position where you are just out of his range. Your strong-side foot should arrive at this third tape line or slightly outside it.

These tape drills are to give you a clear reference for distance and allow you to practice alone when a training partner is not available. Relax and practice the moves up and back until they are quick, strongly balanced, right on the marks, and almost effortless. You should be able to discard the tape markers after a reasonable length of practice time and just "know" the right distance.

Next, enlist training partners with different heights,

reaches, and leg lengths to discover how different body sizes and shapes affect the placing of these distance markers.

Experiment with driving back your training partner with two or three fast sliding-up advances. Try this without hand strikes at first just to get the concept of how fast someone can move back and still maintain balance. You will observe that about the only way a person can move back fast enough to keep the distance sufficiently open to avoid your strikes is by using the slipping-back retreat. Have your partner execute such a drive on you. Note that after two or three fast retreats you start to lose balance. To regain it you must stop moving for a second. This is when you will be hit.

In an actual battle, you may find yourself in a situation where you have slipped your attacker's blow and, having delivered a return strike, are driving on him because he is moving back. Try to learn this timing so that after you have made two or three quick advances you are perceptually ready for that instant of your opponent's immobility as he stops to recover balance. This is the ideal time to blast him with a power strike or to grab and throw him. I found this scenario very common in my bar work.

Indeed, on more than a few occasions, the rapid advance alone caused the retreating opponent to slip and fall without my actually having to throw him. To achieve this, your own balance must be very strong as you move into your man with power and authority. Of course, you must also be able to slip any of his blows as you move in. This includes knees to the groin and attempts to grapple with you to keep his balance and tie up your arms.

Only dynamic practice will teach you the idea behind drive and distance, particularly very light or no-contact free sparring with various training partners of different body types. My pointing out what works, why it works, and how it works establishes a goal whereby you can measure the effectiveness of your training.

CHAPTER 6

GRAPPLING, THROWS, AND ESCAPES

I said many a real fight ends in grappling, and this is certainly true. However, some fights begin with grappling as well.

Lest you think you are too fast or skilled to let some barroom brawler get you in a half nelson, bear hug, or other such hold that requires an escape maneuver, let me relate another incident which occurred to your humble narrator.

Yours truly was going to the men's room to take a piss in a restaurant bar (again, this one wasn't a dive either) when two young kids, maybe nineteen or twenty, both big and clearly in the kind of physical shape that perhaps only nineteen-year olds can achieve, rudely set hands upon me. It was another stupid machismo ritual that I should have just let slide.

We sort of ran into each other as I was going in and they were coming out. One of them blasted the door open on his way out and it almost hit me. I slapped it past me and stepped through. It seems that this maneuver represented some kind of challenge to that delicate,

173

nineteen-year-old mentality. He grabbed my collar to pull me through and out of his way.

The fact is, I just can't get over the idea of people manhandling me. Basically, I tend to respond reflexively when it happens. In this case my reaction was no more than turning the guy's elbow, spinning him around, and tossing him back into the restroom. All this went down in a second, and I saw his companion taking an aggressive stance in his partner's defense.

Now just the three of us were in the men's room. Clearly a tactical error on my part and once again caused by letting my little head do the thinking for my big head. A testosterone attack, so to speak. Still, the guy should not have put his hands on me. I don't do this sort of thing to other people (without reasonable cause, need, or provocation), and I tend to demand the same from them.

The two guys, both larger than myself, not to mention a good ten years plus younger, spread out to either side of me for position. One guy demanded, "You want to fuck with us, man?"

Now, dear reader, after all this good advice I have given you, one might conclude that I responded in the negative to this challenge followed by an attempt to exit. This would have been the correct response for sure. But, like I said, nobody's perfect.

Maybe it had something to do with their youth and arrogance. Maybe it had something to do with my own insecurity and resentment of their youth. In any case, my response was, "Just don't fuck with me, man."

To this the guy replied with the penetratingly astute mathematical observation, "There are two of us." Like maybe I had failed to notice this in the confines of this spacious lavatory.

Again, I acted stupidly—that is, emotionally—rather than logically and tactically. "And you haven't got a fucking chance," I responded calmly. The next microsecond, what do I see? None other than the famous sliding-up advance on my very own person accompanied by a front snap kick to my groin.

The guy executed the move pretty smoothly and very fast. Fortunately for me, he tried to cover a little too much distance and I was trained and alert. His kick connected with the stretched-tight fabric of my blue jeans as I stepped back, and he recovered in a manner that clearly suggested some training. No contact to me at all, but it couldn't have been any closer.

"Gosh, is that the best you can do?" I asked. My idea was to psyche him out with my complete calmness. There was definitely surprise and consternation in his face as he stepped back.

However, while I was playing Mr. Cool with my psych-op remark, the next thing I knew, *bammo*, his pal has me in a half nelson. I felt the youthful arms of steel around my precious neck. Remarkably, the first guy made no move to take advantage of my predicament.

At this point I realized, despite the provocation, that all of this was unnecessary bullshit for which I was, in some part, responsible. Now understand me, a fight is no place for any reflections on right, wrong, or anything else except, as the master swordsman put it, the thought of "cutting and killing your enemy." Only this was not a real fight to me. I didn't ever feel my safety or life were truly jeopardized. The half nelson was strong but, as I will shortly point out, such holds are really the mark of a foolish adversary and are easily defeated.

I knew I could break out of the hold quite easily, but I also knew the move would likely bust the back of the guy's skull against the sink when I threw him. Since he wasn't trying to break my neck, throw me to the floor, or anything else and his pal was not joining in on the festivities, I felt I had an option.

Consequently, I offered the guy who had me in the half nelson an option as well. Very calmly, almost with exasperation in my voice, I said, "Let go or I'll break your back." Don't ask me why I said "back" since it was his skull that would have been fractured. To my surprise, he let me go at once and stepped back. I guess I must have sounded pretty convincing somehow.

I won't test your patience with further details of this encounter. This was the sum total of the action such as it was. We sure didn't put each other on our Christmas lists when we parted, but some measure of mutual respect may have been achieved.

This example is certainly not typical of holds and grappling encounters, but if I can get suckered into such a Hulk Hogan-type move, maybe you can, too. Hence we are going to look at escapes from such holds. First, however, let's consider the objectives and motivations of a person who puts you in such a hold. This knowledge is of tactical value.

There are really only two reasons why a person will try to put a bear hug, full nelson, or half nelson on you. The first is that they want to hold you so that an accomplice can pound on you while you are restrained from defending yourself. The second reason is that they just don't know any better.

You see, in my experience, if the guy is alone and restrains you like this, it is simply a sign of his lack of fighting knowledge or his unwillingness to fight you. These are restraining techniques (if they can be dignified by being called techniques); they are not striking techniques. Do not let this lead you to believe that they are harmless because they are not. A full nelson is illegal in legitimate wrestling (not the television version) because of the real danger of spinal injury and paralysis. You cannot take these holds lightly. Despite my little yarn about the bathroom commandos, you should effect an escape immediately.

Escapes are one of the very few examples of martial arts techniques that will almost always work if you know how to apply them and, most importantly, keep your head and go into the move at once. When a person has a hold on you, then you know in most cases where he is and where the targets are. Things aren't moving too fast at this point. To a large extent, the guy who puts you in a hold has given away the initiative and exposed himself greatly.

The error I have seen most people make when actually put in a nelson or bear hug (front or rear) is conceptually the same mistake many people make when confronted by a Rhino attack. Specifically, they perceive a force being applied to them and try to counter that force with force. They see someone charging at them to knock them off their feet so they try to root themselves in the ground to oppose that force. When someone feels the arms of his assailant on his neck or around his waist, the tendency is to fight those arms. Sometimes this might work if you are stronger than the guy holding you, but I have observed that it is usually the larger, stronger guys that go for these holds. They tend to rely on their superior strength, and getting a hold of someone is their way of applying that strength to the conflict.

ESCAPING FROM THE BEAR HUG FROM BEHIND

While the technique I describe here is effective against a bear hug from the rear, it can also be used against the half nelson.

Observe the photos on pages 179-182. In the first view we see the bear hug has been applied from behind, trapping the defender's arms. (If the bear hug does not trap your arms and the guy just has you by the waist, then you are really dealing with a dildo that is about to hit some hard ground.) The first thing to do is slightly bend your knees in a semihorse stance to stabilize yourself from being thrown to the ground. At the same time, execute a rear head strike.

The rear head strike is no more than tossing your

head forward, then snapping it back into the guy in hopes of impacting on his nose or somewhere on his face (see the second photo on page 180). Believe me, most times it will. The back of your head is solid skull; the guy's face is softer tissue and weaker bones. This means you can land a real knockout shot with little danger of hurting your head. Repeat this strike as many times as you feel it connect. I have had knuckleheads continue to hold onto me while I banged them two or three times in the face. By that time they were out on their feet, and everything else tended to go real smoothly.

In the third photo the defender has dropped down a bit and stepped behind his attacker's right leg with his own left leg. You can step behind the left, too; I just always feel most comfortable going behind the right leg.

Note that at no time is the guy's grip broken or even really contested. Not only does this mean that his being stronger than you does not help him greatly, but while you are making these moves, he still has a hold on you and feels he is basically in control of the situation. He may be gripping down a little harder on you but otherwise that's all he is doing. He isn't doing anything to interfere with your counter and throw.

Here we have the attacker coming from behind with the rear bear hug. This does happen in real battles. There are two reasons a person will apply such a grip: to hold you for an attack by his buddy or simply because he doesn't know any better. If he is holding you for an accomplice to attack, then a front kick may be justified since it can be executed immediately and the guy holding you actually stabilizes you for the kick. Practice this so you will get the correct distance, as the tendency is often to kick the second attacker a little too far away. Experiment with the front snap kick under the chin, too. This is a high kick, but if you practice and the first guy is supporting you like this, then this application of a high kick in a real fight may be justified.

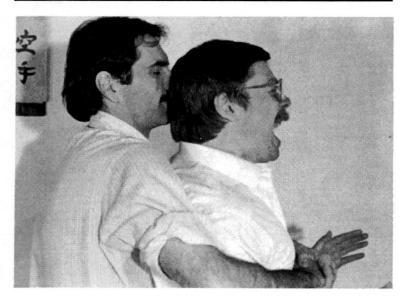

Close-up of a rear head butt (top). Toss the head forward, then snap it back.

The defender throws his left leg behind his assailant's right (right). When done correctly, this does not require any real contesting of the opponent's grip or power. He simultaneously grasps the leg behind the knee; the knees are bent in preparation for the throw.

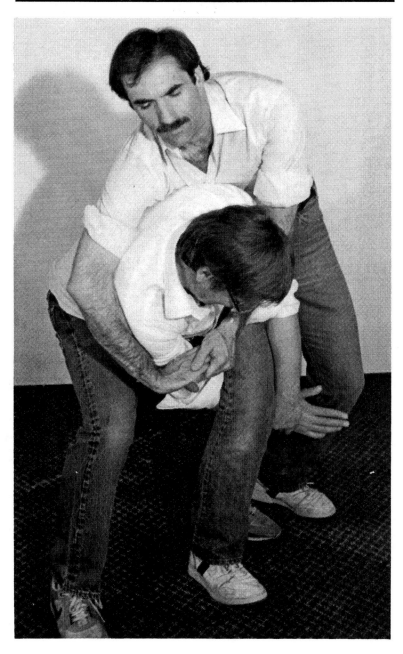

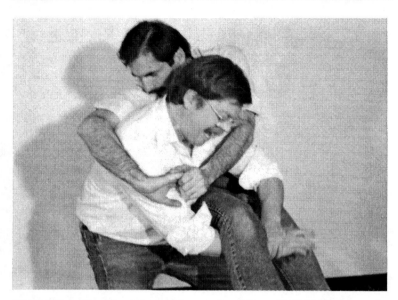

The defender stands up in such a way that the throw is accomplished by the power of his legs rather than his arm strength alone. This is done in the spirit of "throwing the attacker's foot to the heavens." It should be done in a brutally snappy manner. The attacker will most often break his grip in order to catch his fall. If he does not break his grip and instead holds onto you to keep himself up, try "running the mark" by carrying him backward and crashing him into some suitably solid object. If your attacker is too strong or heavy for you to permit this technique, then throw your entire body weight backward, falling with and on top of him. Go for the rear head butt immediately after impact as you break away, then jump up to avoid a floor grappling situation.

Observe the grip the defender employs behind the attacker's knee. You can experiment with other grips and finger locks. The idea is to have a grip that won't break loose under the force of your throw.

The defender bends his knees to lower himself. He holds his grip solid while partially standing up, using the power of his legs rather than his arms. The attacker's foot is lifted off the ground (fourth photo), and the move is completed with a violent whipping up of the leg, which drops the attacker over backward. You may have to duck out of the hold as you throw the guy. Most times this will not be required since he will break his hold in order to catch his fall.

Rarely have I had the guy hang on while his leg was tossed up. If it does happen, it's best to simply fall back with him while trying to make the back of your head hit him in the face when both of you impact on the floor. Remember, he'll hit first and absorb a lot of the shock of your fall. Also, you are choosing the instant of the fall and are much better prepared than he to absorb the impact.

If you have to go down with him like this, the rear elbow strike to the face or hammer fist to the solar plexus or groin are natural strikes. Any blows you strike are done the instant after you hit the floor and are simply made to stun your opponent so you can jump up first. Move quickly to prevent him from grappling with you from behind. Practice on a mat with a training partner and get used to the timing of the impact and your body position in relation to your opponent's after you hit the ground.

In some very extreme cases when the guy was especially gnarly and big and didn't fall when I jerked out his leg, I would run him backward a little (actually carrying him) before dropping myself over and causing his fall. On hard pavement, this technique can be devastating.

The human head is heavy, fifteen pounds or more depending on the size of the individual. This weight tends to give the head inertia that the neck muscles cannot overcome when the shoulders hit the ground solidly and with velocity. The result is that the head flops back and strikes the ground very hard. Be aware that this can be fatal if it occurs on a very hard surface like concrete.

Any technique can go wrong, but this escape is really

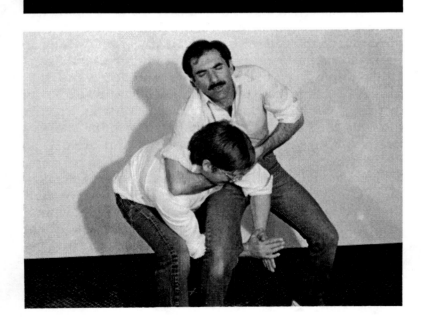

Here we see basically the same defense used against the head lock (top left). The defender executes a snappy shuto strike to the opponent's groin. If you are put in a head lock (or a half nelson), be aware that the attacker has almost always given you a good shot at his groin. The groin strike simply gives him something else to think about while you go for that leg and the throw. You must make these two moves in one flowing, continuous motion. Scream as you move and strike; it may confuse your opponent and tense him up.

Once again, "shoot the foot to the heavens." Note the different grip that the defender uses behind the attacker's leg in this photo and the previous example (bottom left). Experiment with both to see which is best for you.

so straightforward that most of the time, if you keep your head and launch directly into it, it will put your man down. Keep in mind that you do the lifting with the more powerful muscles of your legs, not with your arm strength alone.

Should your attacker let go of you at any point before the throw, continue with the technique without any hesitation. Once he lets go, you are in greater danger because now he can use his hands to strike you.

If the leg gets away from you before the throw is completed and his hands have broken free while you are bent over trying for the leg, then snap up with a blasting rear head strike to his face. Observe the photo where the defender has just secured the leg. If at this point the guy lets go, study why he would be vulnerable to this rear head shot if you reacted immediately upon feeling his hands break loose.

Move slowly at first during training, particularly with the rear head strike, as this blow is rather difficult to control. Experiment with reverse punches to the groin and rear elbow strikes to the throat when studying the mechanics of this escape. Also, study how grabbing the guy's belt at the center of his back can be used as a backup move to effect the throw should your leg lift fail. If this occurs, you have to throw your entire body weight into it and go down with him.

Many martial arts instructors will also tell you to stomp hard on the guy's foot as soon as he grabs you. This is fine, but I have seldom done it. I go directly for the rear head strike.

DEALING WITH THE GRAB

People will try to grab your wrist, your lapel, or most anything else. Sometimes this is meant to stabilize their target (you) before they punch. This can occur surprisingly fast. My only problem with dealing with this has been indecision at the instant it occurs as to what level of response is demanded. The guy could be grabbing ahold to stick a knife into me. On the other hand, he could just be a drunk and acting stupidly. When you are in the bouncer biz, you can't be blasting people with full-force continuous strikes just because they touch you. This was a real problem for me because it tended to disturb my "one mind," or *mushien,* and thus placed a barrier between my intention and actions because I was not sure what action was appropriate.

In general, however, you are safest to blast the guy at once if he grabs you. There may be some legal liability here, but if it comes to a self-defense claim, remember to tell the cops (or the judge if it's a misdemeanor "physical harassment" charge) something like, "I didn't know what he had in mind grabbing me like that. I couldn't wait and see if he was about to stick a knife in me!"

This reminds me of another case I had. (Stand by for further digression from the immediate point.) This big guy, maybe 6'3", but not real heavy, maybe 220 pounds, grabbed ahold of me from my blind side. At the time I was playing peacemaker outside this bar trying to pull my buddy away from a potential fight between him and this other guy.

I was surprised when the guy grabbed me because I hadn't seen him yet. I immediately pinned his hand to my body with my left as I gave him a vertical fist to the nose, a shuto to the side of his neck, and a backfist as he drew away. All were good solid shots, and I actually remember screaming out *kiais* as I hit the guy.

It was kind of funny when I think back on it, but mostly it pissed me off because guess what this slime sucker does after I blast him? He runs over to a cop car that had just pulled up to the bar, doubtlessly called by the management's bouncers because of the battle that appeared to be brewing between my pal and this other guy. (This appearance by the King's Officers was fully expected by yours truly, which is why I was trying to get me and my buddy out of there in the first place.) The guy I hit was yelling, "Help! Help! He's trying to kill me!" to the cops. It was all I could do to hold myself back from finishing off the subhuman slime. I was taken in by the cops but eventually got off with a misdemeanor charge.

It's remarkable how some guys will act so damn tough until you spill a little of their blood, then all of a sudden they're the victim.

Okay, back to the idea of how to handle the grab. At the least, should you be reluctant to blast the guy instantly, step into him as you shoot your hand to his free shoulder (the shoulder of the arm that is not holding you). This is where the punch will come from if that's his intention. Drop your head away at the same time and you should avoid getting a full-force shot should he uncork one.

Now listen real close here. Some people will try to stick a knife in you. They will not display their knife before trying to thrust it into your guts. Therefore, instantly perceive if his free hand is at high or low gate. If it is at high gate, you not only can maybe see if he has a blade, he actually isn't very likely to have one since real knifers don't use an overhead attack very often. *But* if he grabs a hold of you and his hand is at low gate below your vision, this could be a knife attack. You must slap down on his incoming wrist as you turn your body away. Hopefully this will catch his hand before he gets a blade into you. This move can give you that split second to see whether or not you are in a knife fight.

I have had knives pulled on me several times and been attacked with knives three times. Though knife defenses are beyond the scope of this book, I thought I should throw this one out. Remember, knifers most often attack with an underhand thrust from low gate and don't display the weapon before they use it. Expect to be cut in a real knife attack.

The Eagle's Alien

Sometimes people will put their hands on you when they are just trying to intimidate you, like the schoolyard bully who would push his victims on the playground. While simply blasting the bastard might not be fully demanded, you may not wish to tolerate this. Besides, it may encourage the guy to go further. Grabbing onto someone's collar and selling them shit is a form of "hot interview."

Here is a move I was shown by the Amazing Eagle; he calls it the Alien. It is really charming. The Eagle has always been more willing than I to risk problems by not immediately dispatching his assailants. He is also much more experienced at the bouncer trade than I am so he has learned more techniques for controlling people without blasting them.

The Alien is very simple. When the guy grabs you, simply reach up and cover his eyes with your hand. Try this with a training partner but don't tell him what you are going to do when he grabs you. He will break off his grab at once and step away from you. It is almost pure reflex. I have only used this technique once for real and the guy was drunk, but this is exactly what he did. In fact, he stepped back so abruptly that he almost fell down.

ESCAPING FROM THE WRIST GRAB

As Homo sapiens, we are blessed with an opposable thumb. This allows us to grasp objects and hold them firmly. Monkeys have an opposable thumb, too. In fact, some types of monkeys actually make and use simple tools. A straw, stripped smooth, is inserted in an ant hole to withdraw ants clinging to it. The ants are cleaned off and eaten. All this is made possible by that old opposable thumb as well as the more advanced central nervous system.

Our central nervous systems are even more advanced

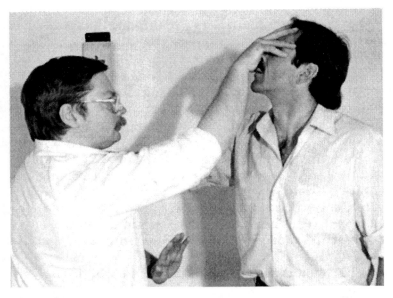

The Eagle's Alien is not a strike, but it is a useful move for your toolbox. It is a method to "back off" a manhandler or drunk who sets hands on you or is about to do same, but who really is not a threat to your safety. The idea is to discourage this behavior without actually injuring him. When you block his eyes like this, the guy will instinctively and immediately step backwards. It really works well on a drunk. This move was taught to me by a more experienced bouncer, Mike H., otherwise known in the trade as "The Amazing Eagle," a living legend in his craft.

than those monkeys (most of us anyway), but when somebody grabs a person's wrist, somehow that superior human brain seems to go on overload. The person feels a restraining force applied to his wrist and attempts to pull away. This is contesting power and thus not the True Way.

You need not contest the person's entire arm and hand strength to break the wrist grab. The only thing that makes his grab work is his thumb. You need only open his thumb from his hand to break the grip. When you use your arm, hand, and wrist power properly, you stack all this up against the opponent's thumb power. I will tell you, even Arnold Schwarzenegger's thumb is not likely to be as strong as your arm, hand, and wrist. But you must use them properly.

I have met only a few people, regardless of size, who could keep a hold on my wrist for more than half a second or so. Those who could were good martial artists, kung-fu guys or aikidoists who would just mirror my movements and maintain the thumb grip. You don't have to worry about guys like that.

You can only learn the move by practicing with various partners holding on to your wrist as powerfully as they can. Here is the basic concept. Instead of pulling away, push forward toward your man, which sets up his muscle group. Then pull towards you and quickly twist your wrist out of his hand by breaking his thumb hold. The movement is sort of a tight twirl of your wrist. Have your partner grip you fairly loosely at first so you can feel the mechanics of applying all your force to the thumb alone.

Your hand will be in rapid motion as you break away, and anytime your hand is in rapid motion is an opportunity to turn that motion into a blow. Experiment with that concept. The vertical fist follows very well from the wrist breakaway. When your hand breaks free it will be drawing into your body, which can chamber this blow. Furthermore, your attacker's attention is caught for a split second by the breakaway. He has only a pitiful chance to block your vertical fist to his nose if it is executed in an immediate and snappy manner. Remember the concept of continuous attack if the situation demands it.

ESCAPING FROM THE FRONT BEAR HUG

Yes, this absurd move is actually used in barroom conflicts, especially by real big guys. It seems that some people are so large, at least in comparison to the general population that they often try to fuck with, that they come to rely almost exclusively on their brute strength. Most of the time they get by without a real fight because they intimidate their victims who don't call them out on it.

If you are smart, you won't call them out on it either unless it is to "fail" the interview. What's really to be gained by it anyway, except maybe some social service by pounding on the bully? This can be expensive for you, though, both legally and medically.

When I have had to mix it up with some of these guys and popped them several times in the head or chin or somewhere real solidly, they invariably tried to tie up the arms that were hitting them. This would begin a grappling situation during which I have had my feet yanked off the floor by such guys.

If this occurs, you are not really in too much trouble if you keep your head. He can't hit you when he has both arms holding you. Grab behind either side of his head below his ears with both hands. Then yank forward on his head as you smash his face with a forward head butt. Repeat same as long as he holds on. You can also break away with the double open-palm clap on both ears just like you've seen in the movies. This is one of those movie fight stunts that really does work fairly well.

The primary danger in this hold is your being thrown down and stomped. Use his body as support by holding onto his neck as described right off the bat. Should your feet still be on the ground or just as he sets you down for a moment, this is an opportunity for the rising knee strike to the groin. Don't expect the guy to fall down writhing in agony from a knee to the groin; most times he will not. You need to repeat the technique a few times to break away.

In any such grappling situation where you are facing the guy, execute the open hand to the throat as a matter of reflex. The sequence of blows shown in the escape from the front choke (pages 47-54) can be used for the front bear hug as well.

ESCAPING FROM THE REAR CHOKE

The rear choke is more difficult to handle than the front choke, but all the principles of defense still apply. The rear head strike comes first. You might follow this with a foot stomp; impact on his instep with the heel of your foot.

Foot stomps should be executed one after another because the guy will move his foot when struck, perhaps raising or turning it and thus giving the next strike more chance to impact in a more damaging manner. When executing continuous foot stomps, *yell!* Old Musashi, that grim swordsman of feudal Japan, wrote in *A Book of Five Rings*, "The shout is a thing of life. We shout against fires and so on, against the wind and waves. The voice shows energy."

Shouting can also distract an enemy, just like when a book hits the floor unexpectedly, making one freeze for an instant. I believe in the *kiai* in actual fighting. I know some accomplished fighters do not (Bruce Lee apparently was one) but what the hell, it's worked for me!

Similar to the thumb break, you do not need to contest the guy's whole arm and hand strength during a rear choke. Try grabbing onto a single finger and wrenching it back with full force. If you haven't broken free with this, the stomps, or the head butts (although you should) and the guy is still cutting off your air, it's time for other measures. Hold your thumb extended slightly from your closed fist and try to execute a few rear thumb strikes to your opponent's eye. If you can, reach back and grab his hair to stabilize his head and give you a better idea where his eye is located. Even if you miss his eye, the strikes should be powerfully and viciously executed so that your thumbnail cuts his face open.

Another approach is to reach behind, slip your hand under his belt, and grab his testicles. This is no time to be shy! If the person is wearing tight blue jeans, you won't be able to get an adequate grip on his balls through the fabric. You must reach inside his pants. Twist and yank his scrotum as you scream out a *kiai!*

Rear elbow strikes to the head and neck help when someone is holding or choking you from behind. They are also good strikes the instant you break the hold.

I have never had to use the rear eye strikes because the stomping and head strikes always broke the choke hold. I have used the old testicle grab, but this was in a grappling situation on the ground. Worked like a charm, too.

Having studied judo and jujutsu somewhat extensively, I know that if a person knows how to put a true rear choke on you, you have a big problem on your hands because you only have a few seconds to escape the hold. Real chokes don't shut off air to your lungs as much as they shut off blood to your brain. This puts you out in seconds. Lucky for us, most people don't know how to apply such chokes.

The kind of rear chokes most people have applied to me have set them up well for a classic judo *ippon*, a forward hip throw. These types of throws are not generally useful in real fights (unless you master them), but the rear choke is an exception because the guy has basically given you the throw. You can only learn this throw under a competent judo instructor (most, but by no means all, are Japanese) so I won't attempt to go into it here.

The one time this throw did not work for me was because the guy pulled my head back powerfully as he applied the choke. This made the throw impossible, but the fundamental judo concept of "when pulled, push" came directly to mind. I drove backward with the power of my legs, which pushed both of us across the floor and into the wall. He still didn't lose his hold, though (one hell of a disappointment for me, I want to tell you). Luckily, I got help from another doorman before his choke put me out. What the fuck, the guy was awfully big.

Sometimes one's training and experience make certain realities so first nature and obvious that one tends to forget their significance or at least that everybody doesn't share this knowledge. The fact that my escape failed from this Conan-type guy in the Iron Blossom Saloon brings this to mind. A Mr. Porche recently brought this fact to my attention with a letter he wrote concerning my training videos. He said, "I now realize that there are no guarantees in real fight situations." This is quite true. As I said at the outset, anybody can get their ass kicked.

THE FUNDAMENTAL THROW: *USOTO GARI*

I studied judo for many years. Judo is the sport of throwing your opponent by using hip leverage. It relies heavily on grasping the judo gi for a grip on your man. Indeed, the contest is principally carried out with both judoka holding onto each others lapels and moving about trying to force an opening for a throw.

Judo throws are done with the power of the legs. The hip is used as the fulcrum. The judoka turns instantly and thrusts his own hip into his opponent. Once the opponent is momentarily on the fulcrum of the hip, the knees are raised, the opponent's feet leave the ground, and he is thrown. Most all of these throws involve turning your back on your opponent at the instant of the throw. This is something you don't want to risk in a real fight unless you are an A-number-one judoka. While I have met judo people who I think could throw just about anybody under just about any circumstances of attack

Usoto gari **is a simple leg throw from the art of judo. It works well in actual fighting situations and is illustrated here in the classical manner. This throw can drop your opponent very hard. In the first illustration, the opponents grapple. Note that each is holding the other with one hand at the elbow and the other hand at the lapel. If your attacker is wearing a T-shirt and there is no lapel to grip, then grab behind his neck with one hand and the inside of the elbow with the other.**

Quickly jerk his elbow down while jerking his opposite shoulder up. This is a twisting motion that shifts your opponent's body weight entirely to the leg that you are about to sweep out from beneath him. Try to step *past* your man with your support leg.

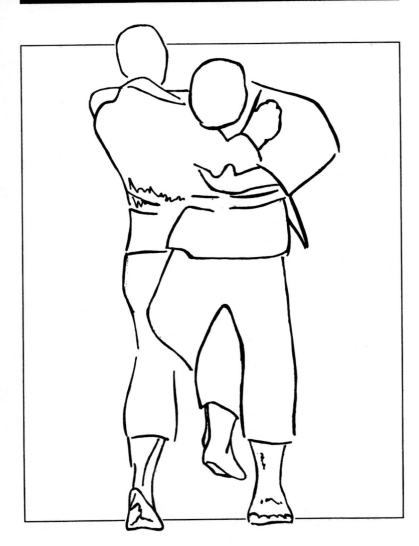

You must strike the back of your opponent's leg with substantial force to knock it out from under him. This is achieved by pitching your entire body weight into him. Your head should drop past his as you throw your body weight past the leg you are sweeping.

The throw is achieved when you knock out his leg. You must commit yourself fully to the throw. Even if it fails it does not leave you too vulnerable to counterattack. The full commitment of your body weight can cause you to fall with your opponent. Consequently, you must practice the technique on a mat with a training partner after you've both learned how to break a fall. Practice will allow you to throw him and stay on your feet.

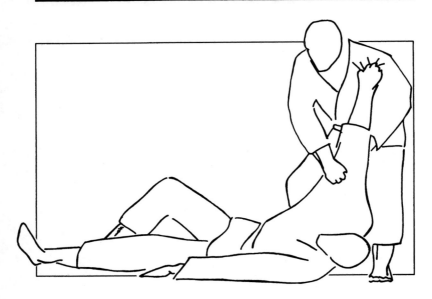

Classical judo training will teach you this throw in a way that can be effectively generalized to an actual battle. Note that the opponent's arm is retained in this drawing. This allows for tactical control through pain-compliance arm and wrist locks. The alternative is to retain the limb just long enough to insure an awkward fall and then let go so the body impacts with maximum velocity.

(Master Yoshishada Yonezuka was one), I feel that the major hip throws of Kano-style judo are not directly applicable to real fights for most people.

Since I am on the subject of formal judo training, I will say that judo is a fundamental martial art you should study. All that *randori* work really drills into you the ability to perceive the subtle shifts of movement and balance that occur in a stand-up grappling situation during an actual fight. This is the critical sense of timing you need to make simple throws and spinouts work in a real fight. Judo training is a very good way to develop this sense of perception. It is also quite demanding physically, and will teach you the very necessary skill of taking a fall with minimum (or no) injury.

The simple judo leg throw that I have used many times in real fights is called *usoto gari*. Executed while facing your opponent, it is little more than whacking his leg out from under him by striking behind his leg with yours as you wrench the top of his body back with your hand. This causes him to fall backwards hard.

When you grab onto the guy's clothing, learn to make an instantaneous twisting motion with your hands that immediately takes up all the slack in his clothing. This is done to make your grip firm and translate your force directly to his body.

Step past your man with your striking leg so that your body weight is past him. Then whip your leg behind his knee, knocking his leg out from under him. Further, try to crash into his shoulder with yours at the same time your leg impacts behind his knee. This is a power strike. Your head should be leaning past his shoulder at impact.

You have to get the timing right. Sometimes you have to rock the guy back and forth before the throw, transferring his weight from one leg to the other. You make the sweep just as his weight is coming off the leg, but this means you must begin the movement just before the weight shift occurs. This demands perception.

This is one of the few techniques that is fully committed. If you go down with him, it's really not so bad. You will be on top of him and his body will break the impact of the fall. When you hit the ground, launch into a continuous attack with a hammer fist to the nose or whatever strike comes naturally.

If you get past him and your leg connects but he doesn't go down, then throw all of your body weight behind him and launch yourself into the ground, dropping your full weight into him and past his balance point. Unless he is very much heavier than you or is short and heavy, he will go down. In any case, you are too close and too much behind him to get punched or kicked right off should the move fail. As a backup, if he just won't fall, go to the horizontal elbow strike to the throat. The open hand to the throat is a good one, too. After impact, immediately attempt the throw again.

This move has worked for me almost every time without having to go to a second attempt or any of the above-mentioned backup maneuvers. But I studied this technique in judo class for many years and it was my favorite throw in sport competition.

THE HEAD AND ELBOW SPINOUT

I think it was the Eagle himself who said, "Where the the elbow goes, the man follows."

The movement I am about to relate is a very fundamental grappling technique. Keep in mind that most fights end in some form of grappling. I don't know if I can get this across in a book, but the description may help you discover the principle when you train with a partner.

Place your hand behind your training partner's neck and your other hand on the inside of his elbow. Slowly pull his head forward as you push his elbow back. Your hands should be tracing out the perimeter of a circle. His head is the center of the circle and his arm is moved around the center at the outset of the movement. You are moving his head into you as his arm is pushed back. Once you get him in motion, the head is turned downward as the arm is thrust up.

At present, we are just talking about the mechanics of the move. How you get all this to happen in a dynamic situation is a matter of perception of the opponent's movement combined with proper timing and authoritative action on your part. All of that, by the way, chiefly depends on proper fighting attitude even more than knowing the technique itself.

I have used this spinout enough to know it is a valuable technique once mastered to some degree. I have mostly used the wrist rather than the elbow. This gives greater leverage. Sometimes, however, I first made contact at the elbow and then slipped my hand down to the wrist as things were set in motion.

Aikidoists have polished this basic move into a handful of core techniques of their art. An aikido or aikijutsu person can show it to you. They may have some embellishment or particular form for it, but basically it's just a spinout.

Keep this concept in mind. When something is spinning, there is an axis upon which it spins. At the center there isn't much movement. At first your opponent is at the center since you have to get him moving. Therefore you begin the motion by moving around him as you pull him off balance. Then, once he's moving a bit, you become the center of the circle as you draw him around the circumference. At this point, your movement at the center is slight, but his is great as he moves around the outside of the circle. It is easy for you to keep your balance, but he has to keep pursuing his. This keeps him moving.

In the real world this technique also depends on some torque. Use your legs to move forward as your hands draw his head into you and thrust his arm (elbow, wrist; they're all connected anyway) in an upward direction.

You learn this technique by trying it out on your training partner, but use reasonable caution and go slowly at first. Experiment with hand positions behind the neck and on the wrist, arm, and elbow. Remember, you are not standing still but moving your whole body briskly around the center of the circle.

Once you get him moving around the circle, there are any number of points from which you can redirect his inertia tangentially. This allows you to direct your opponent into suitable objects when you let go of him.

Alternatively, this spinout can be a short-range affair where the guy's head is driven into the edge of the bar or other solid object. In this case you don't let go of him.

Refer back to the photos on pages 50-54. Here, the spinout follows from the elbow strike to the side of the opponent's neck. This is also an example of economy of movement. Your hand is already up there so use it effectively. Notice that in this sequence, the defender's left hand never leaves the attacker's right wrist. Since there is no nice bar edge available, the defender manipulates the opponent's inertia into the rising knee strike.

There are plenty of useful variations on this move. Most of them are determined by how large a circle you use in the spin and if, and when, you let the guy fly. Experiment in your practice.

RUNNING THE MARK

The few times I have executed this move in real confrontations, I found it to be a heart-warming experience. I think that this is the psychology that the aikidoist is sucked into. Once again, the technique which I will crudely describe here is an application in physical mechanics and kinetics that the art of aikido has polished to its bare essence. (But be warned: when a technique is polished to its "bare essence," there isn't much else left, thus it almost has to be executed perfectly to work right.)

Frankly, like the character in *El Topo* said, I think that "too much perfection is a mistake." This is why I always keep in touch with a little bit of the application of force to make the technique work. I believe this allows me to compensate in the midst of a real-life execution for the little errors in hand position, balance, and so on.

On the other hand, I know that this technique, like the aforementioned spinout, can be executed so cleanly that virtually no force or effort is used at all. This is the aikidoist's goal. For the true aikido man, this is tied up in a spiritual idea of the "Harmony of the Universe," which is at the foundation of the art. I have no problem with all that. It's just that I'm not willing to bet my life on it.

The technique I call "running the mark" is a simple application of inertia. Inertia is the physics concept that says that a body at rest tends to stay at rest until acted upon by an external force, and that a body in motion tends to stay in motion until acted upon by some external force. Gravity is the external force on our planet. It's why your car begins to slow down after you take your foot of the gas (friction is just another expression of gravity).

Once you get something that has some weight (mass) in motion, it takes a little time for gravity to arrest that motion. Think about moving a heavy safe or piano on rollers. It may be a real chore to get the sucker to start rolling, but once you do the real chore is stopping it. This is the concept behind running the mark.

Unlike the dead weight of that safe or piano, people are alive and move under their own power. I may not be able to get a 250-pound safe moving too easily, but I have a good chance of getting a 250-pound opponent moving quite smartly if he isn't careful (which means alert and trained to some extent). This is because he is already in motion in his effort to hit me so he has already started the old inertia ball rolling. All I have to do is redirect that inertia and slightly accelerate or amplify it.

We are talking concept here before we get into technique because without understanding the concept you will never get the technique. On the other hand, this is another move that you must try out with a training partner to begin to understand both how it works and how to make it work.

Note how when we talk concept, there are only a few that keep rearing their squirrelly little heads over and over again. Once you master these fundamental concepts, it becomes easier to learn a new technique because you see at once upon which concept it relies to work. After a while, only rarely will you run into a technique that demands you master a new concept. When you do, it's like discovering a buried treasure.

Let's get back to the technique at hand. Running the mark generally follows some kind of grappling situation. Keep in mind, you can initiate the grappling as well as your opponent. Thus you can close on an opponent after you've slipped his shot and use his inertia to get him "running." Alternatively, after you've stunned your man with some heavy shots, you might have the chance to grab onto him and start moving him across the floor such that he has to continually pursue his balance or go down. The idea is to use your leg and foot movements to effect a shift of your opponent's weight and balance and to continue such a shift of weight and balance such that you pull him momentarily off balance.

When someone is off balance, they must raise and reposition a foot to regain it. This can be done in a split second, but if you deliberately caused this slight momentary loss of balance on an opponent, you know precisely when that repositioning must occur. This means you can continue this movement to prevent him from regaining his balance. This forces him to make a quick series of steps, each of which becomes a little greater in length as you "run the mark."

Once you get your opponent moving like this, he can't do anything but keep running along with it or collapse. It is like jumping from a speeding train. You have to run along side the tracks for awhile before you can stop. Your opponent is completely incapable of launching any sort of attack as long as you have him in motion like this. In fact, he can't even break off the line you are drawing him along. This is the true splendor of this move. Just keep him moving until his course is intercepted by Mr. Wall, Mr. Post, Mr. Automobile, or good old Mr. Bar Edge.

The principal difference between running the mark and a spinout is simply that the spinout runs the opponent in a circular fashion while running the mark takes him along a straight line. All of the other concepts are the same.

Aikido people practice interposing attackers between themselves and other attackers. They run their opponent into the next attacker, which breaks that attacker's gate and balance. This seems okay in theory, but I have never done this in a real fight. I guess if you really had the technique wired you might be able to get away with such a stunt.

On the other hand, there have been times when I got big guys moving like this and they were completely helpless until they collided with the terminal object. Since you still have a hold on the guy's neck, arm, or some other part of his limb, you can make it difficult for him to catch his fall on impact. In fact, with practice you can learn to make such impact real awkward and damaging for him.

Learn how to run the mark. If your perception of the attack is good (*awareness*), it will work like the proverbial charm against most all the variations of the Rhino attack.

Okay you Universal Harmony aikido guys out there, I know all this has occurred to you, too! What I describe here has been termed a version of "gnarlmaster aikido" by one particular wearer of the sacred black hakama that I know.

But really, this move is not at all peculiar to the art of aikido, nor is the basic concept unique to that art. I have seen completely unschooled barroom brawlers use it more than a few times. It's not so polished and elegant as in the aikido dojo, but when is real fighting ever polished and elegant?

CHAPTER 7

SELECTING AN APPROPRIATE MARTIAL ART FOR YOUR PERSONAL STUDY

There are more than a dozen martial arts styles popularly taught in the United States. In this chapter I will offer my views on the primary strengths and weaknesses of each of these systems in regard to their application to actual self-defense. These critiques will involve individual techniques as well as training methods. No doubt there will be something to offend almost everyone.

While this final chapter represents a virtual orgy of arrogance on my part, please do not interpret the next few paragraphs as any attempt to mitigate same. I put it forth simply as some more of my "sound advice."

While I have been in a lot more fights in streets and bars than most people, and though I have studied the self-defense applications of martial arts systems a bit more seriously and to a greater depth than many people, it does not mean that the stuff I'm saying in this book represents some *absolute truth*. All I'm offering is my opinions based on my personal experience.

Furthermore, I am addressing the general case as I

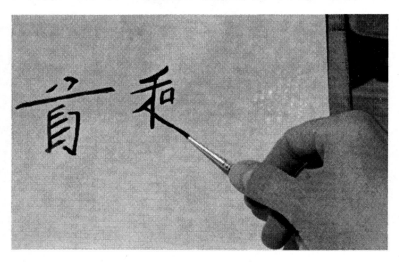

The author acknowledges that his calligraphy is as crude as his martial technique, or sometimes as his life itself. A crude technique for an even cruder world, hence it often works! At left we see the character of the horned head or helmet, which often signifies "Shaman" and is likely derived from the use of antlers on the headgear of a leader or holy man. At right is the character for "harmony" or "heavenly flow of nature." In the art of calligraphy, like the Zen art of the bow (kyudo), we can acquaint ourselves with the principle of "one shot, one life!" Once the brush touches paper, the deed is done, just as in life—no second chance! "One life, one stroke!"

have known it. I am not complicating my points with a discussion of "exceptions to the rule." Exceptions certainly exist. In fact, for every basic position I have taken (such as, "kicking above the waist is generally ineffective and dangerous"), I could have cited an exception to this that I have experienced personally. But why should I? The fact is, as I see it, kicking above the waist is a mistake for most everybody in a real fight. Exceptions only serve to establish the truth of the general principle.

WHY ARE THERE SO MANY
DIFFERENT MARTIAL ARTS SYSTEMS?

There are only so many ways to kick, punch, or throw another human being. So why are there so many different martial arts systems? A related question for the more naive might be, "Which system is best?" Personally, while I do believe some arts are more practical than others, I certainly do not see any one art as being intrinsically superior to all others.

For example, karate (in any of its forms) is not innately better in a real fight than Western boxing. When the karate man fights the boxer, it is not so much these individual arts that will be tested but the *individuals* themselves. Put more simply, it is not so important what styles are being used in the fight as it is *who* is doing the fighting.

However, let's return to this idea of why there are so many different martial arts. An understanding of this will help you select an art (or arts) that are best suited for your personal study.

Basically, there are two primary reasons why martial arts are so varied. First, people's body types vary, and second, people's temperaments vary.

Some people are taller or shorter, bigger or smaller, and heavier or lighter than others. This means they vary in natural speed and brute power as well as in many other attributes. Equally important, people's attitudes vary greatly as to how they feel violence is best dealt with. You have the absolute pacifists on one hand (people who are willing to die before they are willing to kill) and the "Kill 'em all, let God sort 'em out" crowd at the other extreme.

All these different types of bodies and attitudes has caused different individuals and cultures to develop different martial arts. You should take a realistic look at your size, weight, physical strength, and temperament towards violence (this means making people bleed) before choosing a martial art for personal self-defense study.

Here the author engages in calligraphic arts at his home. While traditional martial arts have their limitations in terms of their application to self-defense in our modern world, "there is nothing lost in tradition." Furthermore, training in classical weapons has several practical values. Weapons training develops a good appreciation for angle of attack and evasive footwork. Arts such as kendo (split bamboo sword) or bojutsu (staff) can be quite valuable if you must resort to the use of an improvised weapon or defend yourself against same.

THE SIGNIFICANCE OF BODY TYPE

There are a lot of Chinese people in this world, always have been, and therefore there are a lot of different body types in China. Nowadays there might not be such a wide range in personal attitudes there (seeing as how China has been under Communism for a half century or so), but most Chinese martial arts predate the Chairman's revolution.

The fact is, there are more forms of Chinese martial arts systems than in any other cultural group. These Chinese arts are lumped together in the West under the misnomer "kung fu." There are scores of kung-fu styles, and they can be as different as tai chi is from Western boxing or water polo is from basketball.

A review of Chinese martial arts makes it apparent that body type tends to dictate the appropriate art for an individual. Monkey stylists tend to be smaller, lighter framed, and very quick. Tiger and Bear stylists are heavier, more muscular, and bulky. Each of these styles is designed to take best advantage of the particular capabilities of a specific body type.

In any sport—basketball, high jumping, swimming, boxing—a particular body type will completely dominate. All the players in any given professional sport will have about the same body type except for skin color and other such superficialities. Think about that a moment. You will not see an Arnold Schwarzenegger-type on the basketball court, nor will you see a Magic Johnson in the heavyweight boxing ring.

To further illustrate this point, consider how Western boxing differs in the most fundamental sense from most Asian martial arts. Asian systems use kicking techniques; Western boxing does not. How did this come to be in the first place?

Have you ever been to a museum like the Smithsonian where they have George Washington's wooden false teeth in a glass display along with some of his clothing? Guess you're wondering what the hell this has to do with the price of beans in Yugoslavia, huh?

Well, if you observe that eighteenth-century clothing very astutely, as well as beds, furnishings, and other items from the era, guess what you'll discover? In George Washington's day (just a few hundred years ago), most people were pretty damn short by today's standards. In those days, 5'8" was a reasonably tall guy. A 6' tall guy back then would have been like a Kareem Abdul-Jabbar. (So why is this? Basically because the American diet has improved over the generations. Nutrition is also a central reason why most of our Asian brothers are shorter than Western European types. Beginning to get the picture?)

Have you ever seen a group of small schoolchildren fight? They wrestle, throw each other down, maybe even punch each other. But nobody seems to really get hurt, partly because children have flexible bones, lack the muscular coordination to focus a blow, and are usually not trained in fighting arts. Yet another significant and very fundamental reason why serious injuries rarely occur in these playground conflicts is simply because the children are so small. Without the ability to focus a blow or shift their weight into a strike, children don't generally have enough mass to hurt each other with hand blows.

Now consider this. If in George Washington's day 5'8" was considered reasonably tall, imagine what the average height and body mass of an Asian person might have been centuries earlier when most of the Chinese arts were developed. (Keep in mind that most Korean and Japanese martial arts have their origins in some Chinese form.) If you have a local museum that displays samurai armor of the early Tokugawa Shogunate period (beginning around 1600 or so), you will see that the guys who fit into those outfits were small indeed by modern Western standards.

Because the Asian fighter was a relatively small person, he had to employ the significantly more powerful muscles of the legs in order to do sufficient damage to his enemy in an unarmed encounter. On the other hand, the European, being larger boned and taller, could more easily dispatch his man by using the more easily controlled and focused blows of his fists alone. Thus I believe the principal differences between the Asian martial arts and the Western forms of same can be attributed first to the differences in body types between these groups, and second to their spiritual/cultural differences.

Another aspect of body type affecting the development of fighting styles is that smaller, lighter-boned people can naturally kick better than taller, heavy-boned people. This is simple Newtonian physics. When I say kick "better," I mean faster and with less disturbance to balance, thus allowing for a naturally faster recovery. This is just a matter of smaller-boned, shorter people having to deal with less mass and the fundamentals of inertia. It is not a matter of chance that Thai kickboxers are lighter boned, shorter, and a hell of a lot faster than most Europeans.

Of course with correct and serious training, big guys can learn to kick high and smaller guys can greatly improve the power of their hand strikes, but listen to what a true living master said about martial arts style and body type. I refer to the celebrated jujutsu sensei "Wally Jay" in an interview with Arthur Smith, as printed in *Black Belt* magazine, May 1990: "People are built differently. It's like training a St. Bernard to run; no matter how you train him he will never be a greyhound. So you've got to find what fits you." At the time of this writing, Mr. Jay is 72 years old. He is the innovator of "small circle" judo.

Before I leave this topic of the importance of evaluating your own body type in selecting an appropriate martial art for self-defense study, let me give you some more of Sensei Wallysan's sage council. The late Bruce Lee studied under Mr. Jay. Here Mr. Jay comments on the Little Dragon's view of high kicks in a real fight:

"Bruce Lee did a lot of high kicks in the movies, but he said you should never do a high kick in the street because you can't defend very well standing on one leg with the other high in the air. But he said the public demands such flashy techniques in the movies, so that's why he did it."

Bruce Lee was a martial artist first and an actor second. If anybody could do lighting-fast, well-focused, and instantly recovered kicks, it would have to be our boy Bruce. Note how he was a small, light-boned individual, a body type that lends itself to the high kicking techniques. Yet even Bruce Lee is reported to have said by this unimpeachable source that he would not use high kicks in a real fight.

CONDITIONING YOUR BODY

Regardless of your physical size or body type, you can improve your strength substantially by weight training. Back in the mid-sixties when I seriously undertook martial arts study, lifting weights was considered something that martial artists shouldn't do. The belief was that weight training would reduce your flexibility and slow you down.

This attitude seems to be a thing of the past for many martial artists today. In any case, I have found weight training to be very beneficial to my actual application of fighting techniques to real-life defensive encounters.

Go down to K-Mart and spring for thirty bucks or so for a weight set. You will also need a weight bench, which is also pretty cheap. I paid about thirty-five dollars for mine and it has lasted more than ten years. A weight bench allows you to do bench presses while laying on your back. This is really the best and safest way to use heavy weights. Do not use too much weight if you do not have a spotter to pull the weights off your chest if you overdo it. Consider keeping the weight on the bench rack at all times, too. Then, even if you fail to follow a regular

Weight training is quite beneficial to developing strength. It is largely a myth that it will slow you down or make you "muscle bound." A weight bench is the safest and most effective way to use heavy weight. Do not work out with more than 90 percent of your own body weight. When this limit is reached, do more reps rather than more weight. Note that the author's hands are open, not clenching the bar. This helps train muscle groups such that power muscles can tense for the application of force while tactile/articulation muscles remain relaxed for speed and perception of the opponent's movements. This is especially useful for employing the crane defenses.

workout schedule, just pumping some reps now and then (which you're more likely to do if it's conveniently set up all the time) will show noticeable results fairly quickly.

Like anything else, though, to get the most out of weights you must follow a regular training regime. Measure your progress by the number of repetitions and amount of weight you handle. Don't try to lift more than about 90 percent of your body weight as a maximum. It is not necessary and can cause injury. Do more repetitions rather than more weight. Buy a weight training book to keep track of your progress. It will be fairly rapid at first; then you will hit a plateau.

Try lifting the weights without grasping the bar tightly. This trains the bigger muscles in your arm to tighten for power while your smaller hand and digit muscles remain essentially relaxed. This helps your crane defenses by allowing a relaxed hand and wrist to articulate freely while the arm can tense if the opponent's movement makes this necessary. Again, be careful not to use excessive weight or you may lose the bar.

If you spend just twenty minutes a day, three times a week, in a real lifting workout with enough weight and repetitions to make you strain a little, you will begin to see results in just two to three weeks. Over a period of several months your power will increase greatly. By building up your muscles, you not only will develop greater striking power but you also will increase your ability to absorb a blow to the midsection with less damage. Also, greater arm and back strength helps in grappling and throwing an opponent.

Another exercise device that is useful and economical of your time for the results achieved is the hand squeezer for grip strength. Get one for each hand, and make sure they are stiff enough to make you have to work to close them. The first time you use hand squeezers, your arms will hurt the next day because you are developing muscles beyond what they have been previously used for. A solid grip on my opponent, either on his clothing or body, has been of tremendous value to me in avoiding injury in actual fights.

Running can develop your cardiovascular system to a remarkable degree. I don't like to run but I know it works very well as a training method. Be cautious if you are a larger-boned person, though, as running puts a lot of strain on your ankles and knees. Get a good pair of running shoes, run only on grass or dirt, and don't overdo it or it could come back to haunt you.

An experimental concept in running, especially if you are a lighter-boned person, is to run barefoot. Obviously you will need some soft ground (without broken glass or nails in it) to try this. The first few times I tried it I could hardly walk afterwards. However, it engaged a whole different set of foot and ankle muscles than when I ran with shoes on. Unfortunately, the open pasture I did this in was turned into a subdivision, thus ending my barefoot running experiment.

I imagine aerobics would be a great form of stamina conditioning, but I've never tried it. I just can't deal with a lot of sweating yuppie-types jumping around to music.

While experience has taught me that stamina doesn't always make a difference in a fight that only lasts a few seconds anyway, it is still a big advantage to have good wind. This is especially true if you have to fight more than one guy or the attacker turns out to be a trained fighter who does not go down right away.

A final note on physical conditioning. Guys who bust ass all day in their jobs, like ditch diggers, form setters, and other construction laborers, are often in good shape and strong for their size. Notice the condition of people's hands; it will tell you if they are laborers of this type. I have found such opponents difficult to deal with. They can take a good shot and are real strong in the grapple. Sometimes I think all that hard labor makes them a little mean as well.

THERE'S NO "AUTOMATIC" SELF-DEFENSE VALUE IN MARTIAL ARTS

Before we get into the pros and cons of the specific styles, let me remind you of a fact about all martial arts. They are called arts because that is what they are—*art, not application!*

There is not a lot, if any, inherent or automatic self-defense value in studying a martial art. You must apply the art to real fights yourself. *No fight you may ever find yourself in will ever likely be dealt with effectively with any rehearsed series of movements you practice in the dojo.* Indeed, I recently took an informal survey of some of my martial arts instructor pals, and they all basically agreed that studying a martial art alone does not help most people a whole lot in a real fight.

This is not to say that these arts are not useful, because they certainly are. It's just that *you* must bring the proper attitude to the battle. Proper mental attitude allows you to immediately flow into the appropriate movement when attacked and then to follow through with a proper application of the tools. Without the right attitude, none of the tools you have learned will help you in a real fight.

MARTIAL ART, ITS APPLICATION, AND THE BODY OF A ROCK

Many people study a martial art for its own sake. Their interest is in the art itself and perhaps in the philosophy that accompanies it. A number of these persons have little interest in the application of the art, that is, in developing an effective self-defense ability. Sometimes this is because they are pacifists by nature, sometimes it's because they live in a dream world where they think a real assault can never happen to them, and sometimes it's because they feel they can rely on firearms for their self-defense needs.

I can certainly appreciate art for art's sake. There are some arts I study that have no apparent practical value in the real world. However, to me, the true "art" of the martial system lies quite explicitly in its performance. The measure of that performance in the real world is in one's ability to avoid the conflict but, failing this, to deal with the enemy in a way that precludes his doing injury to you.

Being of the particular temperament that I am, this

latter situation means dropping the sucker to the pavement. But if a martial artist's skill and his particular craft are so strong that they can avoid injury without the necessity of doing serious injury to the attacker, then this would indeed represent the superior craft and the superior artist. As I understand it, this is the ideal of the True Way of aikido.

My objection to those who crowd the dojo with their interest in the art alone (that is, the "art" as they see it; not in its self-defense application) is that they dilute the wine. They pervert things. They clutter the path and can obscure the True Way with a false image. I am not talking about insufficient skill but of insufficient spirit.

The absolute spirit is that of "the body of a rock." This is achieved when one has accepted his death (an inevitability for us all) and thus can think of himself as a "dead body." There is no place left for fear, hesitation, indecision, or any false vision of things. This is the true samurai spirit. We, however, do not live in a world of absolutes, hence it may never be demanded of us to show absolute spirit, the body of a rock.

Even so, without the example and hopefully some measure of understanding of the body of a rock, playing at the art dilutes the art. The shame of this is, when something is diluted, even if little by little, ultimately that something is lost.

WEAPONS HAVE ALWAYS BEEN THE FIRST CHOICE

The use of one's bare hands to defend against attack or to launch an attack has always been a desperation move, a method of last resort, by any people at any time and anywhere on this squalid little planet. It has only been rather recently in mankind's history that the habitual carrying of weapons has become something less than the universal norm.

A significant number of empty-hand Asian martial

arts systems were developed to give the guy who did not have a weapon a chance for survival against an attack from those who did. In the histories of China, Japan, and Korea, there have been prohibitions on who could carry weapons based on social codes, caste systems, or occupation by a military force.

The preferred weapon, prior to the advent of modern firearms, has long been the sword. The sword can be a remarkably formidable weapon in the hands of a person well trained in its use. There are several variations on the physical nature of this tool, but as far as most Asian systems are concerned, we are dealing with some variation of the Chinese broadsword and the classic samurai katana blade.

I bring this up because you should make yourself aware whether or not a particular technique in a given martial arts system was really developed to deal with an attack by a man wielding a sword. This is not to say that the many principles and movements associated with such weapons defenses cannot be effectively generalized to defending against an unarmed assailant. To the contrary, many times they can be. The reverse can also be true; the crane defenses, for example, can be adapted quite well to an attack by a stick or pool cue.

In my opinion, the foundation of certain unarmed defensive arts such as aikido are principally grounded in the idea of an unarmed man moving, redirecting the inertia of, and thus controlling the wrist of a man who is attacking with a samurai sword.

The thing to keep in mind is that a person striking down with a sword or stick in his hand is much more committed to his attack line than a man making a similar movement with an empty hand. Further, it is a bit easier to perceive that attack line. There are also significantly more cues made in preparation of the attack. After all, swords and sticks are weighty things; only a master of the art can wield them as a true extension of his body so that the things I have said here become less true.

Consequently, learn these techniques, but recognize any limitations and how they may have to be modified for dealing with an empty-handed attack. Many of my martial arts buddies will say, "Look, that's the point. This technique was designed to deal with a guy attacking you with a three-foot-long piece of razor-sharp steel. Anything less than that is that much more easily dealt with." From a psychological point of view this is certainly true. It's a lot easier to remain calm and flow into technique when the guy is only throwing a fist rather that slicing at you with a katana. However, the cues are different, the attack line is different, the inertia you are working with is different, and, when a person is holding onto something like a sword hilt, his wrist actions are quite different than when his wrists are "free" to move.

THE MOST COMMON MARTIAL ARTS SYSTEMS AT A GLANCE

There are more than a dozen systems of karate. They can be divided up principally between the Korean and Japanese styles. Keep in mind that karate as it is taught today is really not much more than a century old. Some styles are even younger, with the original founders alive today.

Also, things have changed in the teaching of martial arts. Twenty-five years ago, Asians were the only people who taught any martial arts in this country. Sure there were some non-Asian instructors, but they were rare. There was no big money in teaching martial arts either. Many Asian instructors did it because it was part of their lives and it gave them a way to make a living in a foreign country that allowed them to hold onto a piece of their culture. Schools were much more formal than today. There was much more emphasis on proper behavior and courtesy. It may just be nostalgia on my part, but there was something special about those Asian-instructed schools of the sixties. (I will admit, however, that there was some abuse of the "Asian clans" when it came to tournament judging and such.)

Now we have a Circus Maximus in the martial arts world. It's a commercial deal, with strings of franchised schools like McDonald's that compete with other commercial chains. This has led to very distasteful behavior. There are people instructing martial arts today, and notable ones at that, who my old sensei would have bounced out of his dojo and into the street for their sheer rudeness and arrogance. The old slant-eye could have done it, too.

There was a time when being awarded a black belt was very difficult. It took years of study under a sensei who sometimes deliberately would test your patience and self-discipline. You just didn't memorize some katas, display some techniques, maybe break a few boards, and thus "pass a test" to get a black belt. Yes you had to do all that, but if the instructor did not think you could fight in a full-on balls-to-the-wall alley altercation, then you did not get promoted to black belt. Nowadays I see "black belts" everywhere who know techniques and can do katas okay, but simply cannot fight.

Taekwon-Do

This is the major Korean martial art and the most practiced form of karate in the world. It is a power style with emphasis on kicking over hand techniques. Training is quite uniform in every taekwon-do school. There is a strong emphasis on kata, a series of stepping, blocking, and striking movements performed solo against imaginary opponents. The concept of kata exists in all forms of karate regardless of nationality. Each kata is directed toward a certain belt level and is a prearranged sequence performed the same by everyone in every taekwon-do school in the world. Kata are called *hyung* in Korean.

A typical taekwon-do class involves all the students executing a single kata in unison, with everyone yelling out the *kiai* at appropriate points in the kata. It is performed under the direction of the instructor, who calls out the Korean name for the next move. Punching is also practiced as a group.

Taekwon-do allows free sparring, and many schools now use pads to allow more contact. Blocking in the Korean form is mostly the direct power approach. Great emphasis is placed on powerful blows and equally powerful blocks. Only in the higher black-belt levels does one begin to see circular blocking or slipping of blows such as I have presented in this text.

Personally, I find taekwon-do powerful when mastered but on the whole too rigid and somewhat inapplicable to a real fight. Perfect linear form, straight shoulders, exact foot placement, and the like are emphasized. Such mechanics are of value in a real fight only if your opponent is fighting the same way. The thing is, nobody fights like that. In general, taekwon-do students get a distorted idea of what is involved in an actual fight.

So as not to seem as if I'm grinding my ax too much against the Korean form of karate, I will say that most formal, classical karate styles share these same faults.

A perpetual debate among classical and "new age" fighters concerns whether or not kata is of any value in preparing someone for a real fight. On the whole, I think that it is not. The only real value I have seen in mass drills of reverse punching or sequenced kata is that some students who lack a strong spirit are helped in this because they can identify with the power of the group. They feel their punch carries the power of the whole class as everybody shouts and moves at the same time.

To be fair, I must say that I had one such student tell me after a fight he won that he felt he could actually hear the whole class shouting *kiai* as he struck his attacker. In this person's case, the kata training and mass drill obviously helped, but it was his attitude that was strengthened by this practice more than his technique.

The strongest element of taekwon-do is its emphasis on power strikes. If they connect, they can break bones sometimes. One of its weakest elements is an overly rigid training method that restricts personal style and technique development until black-belt level. Secondly, there is an overreliance on force rather than an understanding of the value of not contesting power. The downside of power blocking is if it fails, it leaves you very rooted and exposed to your opponent's blow. The Korean power approach is too much of an all-or-nothing affair for me.

Finally, kicking is much too strongly emphasized, especially the flashy high kicks, which are not suitable for actual self-defense. This emphasis on the kick leaves the student painfully deficient in the more useful hand techniques such as the slipping and redirecting approaches of the crane. Throws are only superficially dealt with; instead, fancy drop sweeps are taught. *Never* drop to the ground to execute any technique in an actual fight unless it is to duck bullets.

Despite all this, there is a lot to learn about how to punch and kick from taekwon-do. It is sort of a "core discipline" in martial study. You would not have made an error to undertake a study of this art, but keep in mind the realities of actual fighting that I have pointed out all through this book.

Taekwon-do is ironic because this power approach is best suited to big guys with a lot of natural power. However, such big-boned people are just the ones who are least suited to the heavily emphasized kicking techniques of the art.

Tang Soo Do

This Korean form of karate is a bit less rigid in training methods than taekwon-do, and I think a little more practical about real fighting, too. Our hero, Chuck Norris, is a tang soo do man, although he also studied taekwon-do. Tang soo do schools give a bit more time to hand techniques and are a little better about teaching you to throw effectively. While these schools are well-disciplined, I have found them more receptive to allowing students to experiment with techniques.

Nonetheless, while a bit more circular than taekwon-do, this style is still very big on kicking. The tang soo do boys love their spinning back kicks.

Hapkido
This is sometimes called the integrated Korean art because it places a more balanced emphasis on throws, joint locks, and hand techniques as well as on power kicking. This art can be considered one of the more practical of the Korean systems of self-defense. It has similarities to tang soo do, but hell, like I said, there are only so many ways to kick, punch, or throw somebody, and that's what any style of karate is principally about.

Japanese Karate: Wado Ryu, Gojo Ryu, Isshin Ryu, Shotokan
The Japanese karate forms are less power oriented than the Korean forms. They tend to put greater emphasis on circular hand techniques for defense. The Japanese forms are not so rigid with their training methods as Koreans.

While the Japanese forms of karate are naturally similar to the Korean forms, I personally find the atmosphere in dojos that teach the Japanese styles somewhat more pleasant. This depends a lot on the individual instructor, of course.

Wado ryu was the first style of karate that I studied to an advanced level. It was founded by a student of the legendary Gichin Funakoshi, namely O' Sensei Hironori Otsuka. It is a recent style, begun in 1939. Otsuka was a master of shindo yoshin-ryu jujutsu and incorporated some of the Funakoshi forms of karate into this discipline.

The emphasis in wado ryu is much more circular and softer than Funakoshi's style of shotokan. It also places emphasis on smooth and flowing throws. Wado ryu means "harmony way." I have found this curious, as sometimes I can see how wado ryu—if one took certain concepts in the art to the exclusion of others and then refined those to the maximum—is something very much like aikido, which means "way of fundamental harmony with spirit of universe." This may be of little interest to some of you, but the rules say you are supposed to mention your founder's name, his sensei's style, and such when talking about the art. So, okay, I just did.

In my years of wado-ryu study, I have only had to deal with one asshole. In the true spirit of the art, I let the incident pass.

Okinawa is part of Japan, people. In fact for the most part, Japanese karate actually began on the island of Okinawa before coming to mainland Japan. Okinawan karate styles sometimes teach weapons use. They are not quite as sport oriented as other Japanese forms. Some of the Okinawan schools place real emphasis on applied self-defense skills.

Another Japanese style that I have found interesting is

Enshin karate as taught by Shihan Joko Ninomiya. I have not had the privilege of receiving instruction from this master, but I have watched his students in more than a few full-contact matches. They show great spirit and seem to have a particular appreciation for perceiving the angle of attack, not contesting power, and slipping rather than blocking blows. These Enshin karateka would know how to fight if it came down to a real-life encounter. The principal school is in Denver, Colorado.

Shotokan is a power style similar to but not quite as rigid as taekwon-do. Japanese and Koreans sometimes just don't get along well.

Japanese-oriented martial arts schools will often have competent judo or jujutsu instruction available, too. This is something to consider when researching and selecting a school in your area.

Judo
Judo is the sport of throws. The primary throws are done by slamming your hip into the opponent while your hands pull on his gi such that you get him partially on your hip while your knees are slightly bent. The throw, that is the lifting of the opponent off the ground, is done with the legs as you "stand up." The hip is the fulcrum or leverage point for the throw. Other throws include the simple leg throws that we looked at such as *usoto gari*.

There is no punching or kicking in judo. It is a sport where two people hold onto each other and jockey around to create or discover an opening for the throw. The opponent is thrown in a way that is meant to avoid injury to him. Other techniques taught include chokes and "mat work," which is grappling on the ground and getting your man in holds. *Kasa katame* is the basic pin.

Judo is greatly underestimated as a self-defense art by people unfamiliar with its study. I would place judo in the arena of a "core study," just like any of the karate styles I have mentioned. This is because judo teaches you

effective grappling skills that depend on perceiving shifts of body weight before they are completed and a fine sense of your own and your opponent's balance.

Judo training can physically fatigue you to the max. A typical judo class involves *randori*, which is a form of free sparring without blows. The judoka pair up and move around the mat holding onto each other trying to get the throw. If you like to wrestle with an attacker rather than trade punches, judo study will help you do it right.

Judo is not regimented like karate. It is more informal, personable, and friendly in its teaching approach, and judo people tend to have good, friendly attitudes. You don't see as many macho madmen (read *assholes with attitudes*) in a judo academy like one sometimes does in karate schools.

While the hip throws are at the core of judo, I have rarely used them in actual fights even though I studied the art seriously for several years under a strong Japanese instructor. One reason for this is judo does rely somewhat on the costume, the gi, for grabbing. There have been a handful of encounters, however, when someone grabbed onto me in a grappling situation while wearing the old M-65 field jacket or a leather motorcycle jacket and the classic judo hip throw just appeared. Otherwise, I don't believe in turning my back on my opponent in a real fight. He has to give me the throw before I'll go for any major *ippon* like the hip throw. Leg throws are different. They are executed while facing your man and work well if done properly in real fights.

However, I feel judo must be combined with punches and other striking techniques that will soften up your man for the throw. Jujutsu combines the throws of judo with the strikes of karate. In jujutsu, though, hand strikes are more emphasized than fancy kicking techniques. This sets it apart from hapkido or tang soo do.

I mentioned that most fights end in grappling and that judo will teach you practical grappling skills. After you have practiced judo for a few years—which means that two or three times a week you spend an hour and a half or so grappling with a bunch of different body types—your body will respond immediately when a real fight goes to the grapple. It's all old hat to the judoka. You will not be easily thrown by such unschooled attacks like the Rhino. Yet when your opponent makes that first entry into the transitional balance position, *bammo*, you are on it like stink on shit and he is thrown. I like judo but, like any art, it is not complete unto itself.

Learn to protect your groin from knee strikes while grappling. These aren't used in judo, of course, but are favorite moves in a real grappling fight.

A final word on judo for real fighting. The judo throw can be effective where the karate punch or kick may not be. This can happen when your opponent is so much larger or stronger than you that, even though well-executed, your blow does not injure him sufficiently. Not so with the judo throw! If you execute it properly, he is thrown and that is that. In a nasty situation you can make him fall real awkwardly so that maybe he isn't going to be able to get up real soon and continue his nastiness.

This is why judo is real well-adapted to and a good foundation art for shorter, stocky guys. Their lower center of gravity makes it easier to throw the hip into the opponent and get the throw. I have known a few real strong (read *fanatical*) judo guys who stood no more than

5'6" and could throw anybody not schooled in the art and most who were. Even if you weigh no more than 150 pounds, you can learn to throw a guy who tips the scales at 250 if you learn your judo technique well. Being a tall, strong guy doesn't hurt any in the study of judo either.

I think I have used some judo fundamentals in almost every real fight I have been in. Still, keep in mind that your study of judo is really the study of a sport. It is not set up to teach you to fight. You must apply the particular tools of judo to the fight scenario yourself.

Aikido

Before I get into this one, I must tell you that I have never undertaken any real study of aikido. However, after studying various karate, judo, and weapons arts for a number of years, and in light of my actual experiences in observing real-life attacks and defending against same, I presume to grasp what the aikidoist is trying to achieve as well as the manner in which he feels he can achieve it.

I have seen enough aikido performed by competent aikidoists to know what the basic techniques are. I have had the chance to "play around" at attacks with aikidoists; The Amazing Eagle, once a gojo-ryu karate man, now stands among the ranks of aikido acolytes and wears the sacred black hakama. Nish! May his tribe increase. The Eagle rarely passes up an opportunity to enlighten me to the true glory of his art.

There is no punching or kicking in traditional aikido. The throw is at the heart of the art, but this is not the judo-type hip throw at all. Instead, aikido takes the idea behind the technique I called "running the mark" to its ultimate refinement. Aikido also has the virtue of a penetrating appreciation for the principle of not contesting an opponent's power. Aikido does not use power in any significant sense; instead it channels and redirects the opponent's power.

Aikidoists do not try to destroy their enemy; they only

seek to neutralize the attack. The key concept in the execution of an aikido technique is often called "capturing the lead." This means perceiving the opponent's body motion (". . . the body tells," Hollywood Bob) and discerning the tool being used and the angle of attack. This allows the aikidoist to "blend" with the attack and redirect his opponent's inertia for the throw or drop fall.

Much emphasis is placed on wrist manipulation combined with getting some other leverage point on the opponent's body. This other leverage point is often either the elbow, neck, or head. Aikido movements are flowing and circular in nature and the attacker is often "spun out" and sent flying across the room. Centrifugal force is used in some techniques to get the opponent's body moving.

I think a central essence of this art is getting the opponent moving across the floor in such a way that he is continually trying to recover his balance, which the aikidoist keeps just a half step ahead of him. The opponent is controlled by the aikidoist moving across the floor with his leverage points (hands) on the opponent while drawing him around the circumference of a circle. The aikidoist is at the center of this circle so he is stable, but his opponent is moving ever more quickly to capture his balance to avoid stumbling and falling. This control allows the aikido man to accelerate his opponent's motion and, if he wishes, to spin him out tangentially as he lets go. Alternatively, aikido people are famous for the old clothesline to the throat, which is accomplished by holding out a hand or wrist that the opponent collides with at throat level.

Aikido also makes much of nerve pinching techniques in the wrist as pain-compliance moves. These techniques are often employed after the opponent has been brought to the ground. They are fantastically painful. They cannot be escaped from as far as I can see, but the aikidoist has to get one on you first.

While I have not practiced aikido, I have certainly used its principles in running the mark or with the spinout, so I know the techniques can physically work in real fights. But they really must be practiced to a very high level of proficiency to be applied with success in an actual attack. This does not mean you cannot achieve such proficiency.

There are many things I like about aikido, and many of the concepts (keep in mind the difference between concepts and techniques) are very much a part of my personal style. In fact, these same concepts (apart from the some of the spiritual ideas) are pretty similar to judo. Even a few aikido and judo techniques are similar when it comes to restraining holds. But fundamentally, aikido is very different from judo.

What do I see as the central weakness of aikido training as adequate preparation for dealing with a streetfighter? Go back and read about the Hawthorne Effect in Chapter 2. I think many aikido practitioners suffer from this type thinking. When I say to my aikido friends, "I do not think most of the people in your class could effectively apply these techniques in an actual attack," they respond, "Perhaps, but isn't that true of most people who study any form of martial art?" I must confess that this is true.

Aikido is esoteric. The people who study it are basically nonviolent. The atmosphere of the aikido training hall is one of cooperation, respect, and nonviolence. I have never met an aikido person who had a negative attitude or tried to prove he was a tough guy.

Aikido is well-suited to this type of temperament. If you dedicate yourself to the study of this art, it can be very useful in a real attack situation. But as in any art, you must have correct attitude as well as a mastery of the tools. In aikido, this means a truly relaxed mind under attack. The techniques depend on a subtlety and tactile feel that is compromised by either mental or physical tension, and they must flow dynamically and with near perfect timing.

Like judo, there is no fundamental reliance on power and physical strength in the execution of techniques. This is even more true in aikido than judo. In judo, a little upper body strength can sometimes be used to compensate for small errors in execution. But with aikido techniques, physical strength is simply not very relevant. Thus the combination of the aikido temperament with the lack of the use of strength to make things work make this art a more suitable choice for women.

Once again, I think that aikido has merit, even though some call it the "nonfighting art" (in fact, be prepared for an extra dose of hocus-pocus spirituality). However, the dynamics of the movements must be combined with the *atemi* (striking) techniques. Further, the self-defense application must be made by you. If you can get a guy running with an aikido move, then you can just as easily run him into a wall or a passing automobile if the circumstances demand it.

This art, if mastered, may be the best way to deal with weapon attacks (that is, except having a better weapon of your own).

If you are an individual of great spirit, but perhaps of less than great size or physical strength, you may wish to consider aikido.

Kung Fu: The Chinese Systems of "Karate"

It isn't truly correct to call these systems "Chinese karate," but they do mostly involve punching and kicking techniques like the Korean and Japanese forms (which, as I mentioned, likely had Chinese origins).

There are far too many Chinese systems to enumerate. Even so, it is difficult to find truly legitimate instruction in any kung-fu style unless you live in an area with a large Chinese community like San Francisco. Be aware that there are more phony kung-fu instructors than any other martial art. It's rather difficult to pass yourself off as a taekwon-do or shotokan expert if you aren't one because there are enough of those stylists around to expose your fraud rather directly. However, should I call myself a teacher (sifu) of wa shu fan kung fu, I don't generally have to worry about some real wa shu fan man stumbling into one of my classes. This situation, combined with the mysticism that television and movies have associated with kung fu has given rise to a crop of take-the-money-and-run kung-fu teachers. Only thing is, sometimes they keep the charade going for years.

Okay, maybe we are grinding another ax here. There was this guy who presented himself as kung-fu instructor for a few years in the town where I lived and taught classes. Fine with me. Hell, I'll always look in on someone else's style with an eye to learning something new.

But in this guy's case, there wasn't anything to learn except what assholes some people can be. I was polite so he let me watch the class. I did not see anyone who in my opinion had any real fighting skill. I suspected he'd maybe read a few books, seen every episode of "Kung Fu" ever made, and perhaps had some instruction at sometime, somewhere, probably from someone just like himself.

He used his "class" to run a long diatribe on the strength of his "system" over old-fashioned karate, which, of course, was simply a hollow reflection of the

Original Art, which he taught. He spared little in his discussion of the "masters" he had studied under. It was kind of embarrassing to listen to all this so I bowed and left.

A few weeks later the story gets back to me about how this guy had decided that wado ryu was no good, that I would be helpless against him in a fight, and that my students were being trained ineffectively. Now, most times I'd just ignore such nonsense, but you see, the commercial aspects of my getting all his students in my class worked on my mind a little. Besides, the guy had sort of gotten under my skin.

I went back to his class sometime later and waited through the whole charade until all his students had left. You see, I do have some class—I didn't want them to take my actions as an example of how to handle things. Telling the guy I was curious about his art, I asked if he would consent to a match with me which would exclude maiming strikes, bone or joint breaking techniques, and the like, but would permit moderate contact. There was no one else there and he tried to worm out, but I wasn't about to let him off the hook. He had to agree or confess right there.

He actually took one of those David Carradine stances and hissed a little before I punched his lights out. That's how much people can convince themselves of their own fantasies.

You guessed it; a short time later the story gets back to me about how he kicked my ass. The funny thing is, I had never even mentioned the "fight" to anybody. It didn't help much financially either, as I only got one of his students. I just let the whole thing slide as an amusing introspection into human psychology.

So be aware, this was not the only kung-foolishness "instructor" I have run across. Legitimate kung-fu teachers are generally, though not exclusively, Chinese. If they are not, at sometime or other they at least should have studied under a Chinese sifu. You don't become a teacher of any system after just two years or so of study, either.

The kung-fu styles as taught by legitimate people that I have seen divide up into three general categories. There are the soft, flowery styles that seem to have no real application to actual fighting (Nine Dragons at Sea). Then there are the styles that look a lot like the former, but actually have a few really useful moves (if you can hang out long enough and have the experience to spot them). The third type looks a lot like any other karate style, with just a few strange forms here and there. The point is, you not only have a greater chance of ending up with a phony instructor in studying kung fu, there are some styles that have become entirely symbolic dance forms, which are not really martial arts at all. An example of this is tai-chi chuan, only tai chi doesn't try to pretend that it is a fighting art.

The two kung-fu styles that I have had legitimate instruction in are wing chun and white crane. I discovered these styles by being polite and asking if I could watch, and I did just that without making any comments whatsoever. After awhile, I found a Vietnamese and a Chinese instructor who both seemed like they had some good moves that were new to me as techniques but familiar as concepts. Once I got to know them, they agreed to teach me the techniques I was interested in. I certainly never learned any of these styles as systems but I did get a handle on a few useful moves.

In wing chun I discovered the power of the backfist, the usefulness of close-in continuous elbow strikes to the head and throat, and blocking at the source of a punch (shoulder). White crane offered the fundamental technique for slipping a blow that I have attempted to communicate in this book.

There is another kung-fu art I have briefly run across through a student of a guy who I think was named Scotty Wong, who taught in New York City of all places. The guy I sparred with called the form jow ga. I never met this Mr. Wong, but his student was tough. He really went after me and I was hard-pressed to keep him from hurting me. It wasn't his techniques so much as his tenacity, perception, and control of distance. He liked to fight in real close just like I do, only this dude was forcing yours truly to open the distance.

The guy gave me the philosophy of his art, such as it was. It basically came down to the training method being designed to cultivate "killer instinct." Seemed like it worked pretty good to me, so if you happen to find a jow-ga kung-fu school in your area, maybe it's worth looking into. I would not want to have to fight that guy for real, I can tell you that.

There is a style of kung fu for every body type, but make sure your teacher is legitimate and is teaching a fighting art and not a cultural artifact.

Jeet Kune Do: The Fighting Philosophy of Bruce Lee
The best source of information on Bruce Lee's fighting

approach is found in his book, *The Tao of Jeet Kune Do*. Get a copy of *Black Belt* magazine or *Inside Karate* and you will find an ad for this book available from Ohara Publications, Inc.

Bruce Lee is revered in the martial arts world almost to the point of nausea. I take that back; actually he *is* celebrated to the point of nausea. However, when I study *The Tao of Jeet Kune Do*, it is clear to me that Lee was an extraordinary individual. His knowledge of fighting principles was astounding. In fact, it is often the very depth of his observations that make his book somewhat incomprehensible to most people.

Although a student of various kung-fu styles, principally wing chun, Bruce Lee was the first notable Asian martial arts master to challenge the classical methods of training in regard to their application to streetfighting. He coined the term "classical mess." This was simply unheard of at the time Lee did this, the mid-sixties. It was practically a sacrilege to challenge the classical martial arts in any way at that time. Fortunately, things have loosened up a good deal since then.

Bruce was an innovator. He spoke out honestly and irreverently about things as he saw them. He apparently was also an unbridled egomaniac. But what the hell, I can relate to that.

Furthermore, Bruce was remarkably fast in every sense of the word in which I have defined speed. His body coordination was abnormally high, as was his dedication to the art. This means he could make techniques work that some people will never be able to do no matter how much they may study and practice. Such people need to study techniques that are better suited for them, and this is very much part of the jeet kune do concept.

Listen to this quote from *The Tao of Jeet Kune Do:* "Freedom discovers man the moment he loses concern over what impression he is making or about to make." Of

course this is simply a rephrase of an essential Zen parable, but such statements by Lee are profound truths and I feel he meant them sincerely.

Lee was concerned that if he founded a style, people would corrupt and commercialize it. This has occurred to some degree. Lee's jeet kune do is no more than a complex of fundamental concepts that encourage the student to research and discover what works for him. The jeet kune do student will take any technique from any system if he thinks it can work for him in a fight.

After Lee went to that Big Rice Paddy in the Sky, a number of his students and even some casual acquaintances naturally made some effort to establish themselves as the head of jeet kune do. To me this is a reasonable commercial move, but it should not be taken too seriously. There can be no "head" of jeet kune do. In fact, in an important sense, there is really no such art as jeet kune do.

Legitimate schools following this doctrine of study as put forth by Bruce Lee are few and far between. The primary gurus of this cult are Dan Inosanto and a guy named Paul Vunak. I suppose a clue to the authenticity of a jeet kune do school may be some relation to either of these two men. This is not to say that a JKD school cannot be legitimate without some tie to one of these men. Basically, who really knows?

I have had the pleasure to briefly deal with Dan Inosanto (in a seminar with about seventy other guys) and another Filipino stylist, Remy Presas. Both of these guys are very strong fighters. Inosanto is not a young buck anymore (neither am I) but his weapon skills, particularly with the blade, can be rightfully considered legendary.

Do not confuse what you see in *Enter the Dragon* or *Fists of Fury* with jeet kune do. Keep in mind what Wally Jay said that Bruce told him about high kicks in real fights. Also, keep in mind that as strong a martial artist as Bruce was, he died rather young and just wasn't on the planet long enough to see every approach to the problem of unarmed combat.

Even having said this much about jeet kune do and the Deceased Dragon, I'm sure I will have offended plenty of JKD fans. Once again, get a copy of Bruce Lee's book, *The Tao of Jeet Kune Do*. It is a masterful work.

Western Boxing

One of the big advantages of Western boxing is that there are plenty of places to train. Almost every YMCA has a boxing program. Some police departments still have boxing courses to teach juvenile delinquents self-discipline concepts and that all cops aren't the enemy. On top of this, just open your Yellow Pages to Boxing Instruction or Gyms.

Boxing gyms stink a lot because everybody sweats a lot. This is because they train a lot. They train hard, too. Boxing is not for the pink tofu crowd. Boxing hurts. They hit you in the face with leather gloves and they know how to hit, too.

Maybe I shouldn't sugar coat it like this. Boxing is not for the weak in spirit. It is rough training and much more brutal than most Asian martial arts (as taught in the United States anyway). Bleeding is a near regular affair in some boxing gyms, but in a typical Asian dojo, bleeding

means an accident. This is why I think boxing is another "core discipline." It is frequently carried out full contact with gloves and head gear. When I started taking boxing lessons, I was already a seven-year student of both karate and judo. Some of the guys in the gym knew about this and decided this was cause to beat the hell out of me with a little extra furor, which may color my view of boxing training to some degree. In fact, boxing showed me that just because I was practiced in an Asian system, I couldn't necessarily drop the boxer even if I was allowed to use all my moves.

Full-contact training like this teaches you two important things that are much more difficult to perfect in Asian martial arts schools. The first is getting used to being hit hard in the head and not letting it put you away or cause you to stop defending yourself. Boxing not only teaches you this, but it trains you for the instinctive counterpunch. The second thing boxing helps you perfect is how to chain your blows in combinations.

Understand, there is more to this art than just throwing one punch after another in sequence. In boxing, since you actually hit the guy in the head or gut with full force, his body reacts in a similar manner as if it were a streetfight and no gloves were worn. This means you can learn the combinations better because you get a realistic body response to what happens when a blow contacts with power. Such feedback is absent in most dojo training.

One of the first things I saw was that when I connected with a good reverse punch to a guy's solar plexus or abdomen, his head would pitch forward every time. It was just a matter of how much. This was just the motion I needed in a real fight to start the head and elbow spinout and/or the knee to the face or gut. Of course, none of this is legal in boxing, but the sport showed me some good ways to set up a lot of jujutsu moves and some karate blows. (Curiously, I think some people study aikido with a partial eye toward how the moves can set up the hand blow or other *atemi* strike.)

I think one reason boxers tend to be so tough is that the people who aren't tough drop out of the program pretty early. That leaves the people you will find in the boxing gym; that is, guys who can soak up and dish out a beating.

Despite all this, boxing does have some weak points as far as real fights are concerned. These all stem from the prohibition on illegal techniques in the ring and the protection a boxing glove gives one's hands.

I have already stated that you generally cannot hit someone in the skull with your closed fist without risking broken bones or split knuckles. Yet, now that I think about this, I guess the few times I had a serious fight and was wearing my rawhide bike gloves, I must have looked more like a boxer than an Asian-style martial artist because of all the closed-hand shots to the head I threw. The fact is, hands are real accurate, powerful, and naturally easy to focus.

In fact, the aforementioned Eagle has accused me (only half seriously, I hope) of only having one technique, the right hand to the head. But when we spar, it is with gloves on, which is why I can get away with it. I know I can't afford this type of strike with a bare hand and neither can you. I use it against trained fighters in sparring matches using gloves because it is so fast and powerful that it gives me a better chance to land it against them.

If you are a boxer type, keep this in mind. Move in close, work hard on the guy's gut, then go to the head with the backfist or palm-heel shot to the throat. I know this is real hard because the boxing strokes become so instinctive and natural that the left hook or right cross just "pops" up as required. This is why you have to do a little training in the alternatives.

In any case, if you work on the guy's body, it can set him up so if you then go to his head you have a bit more time to see that the blow lands correctly. This helps prevent injury. If you just can't get away from using a closed fist to the guy's head, the chin (using the cross or hook) is a safer target.

Boxers can sometimes be dropped by knee strikes to the groin in a clinch, but don't count on it. I think such knee attacks against the boxer are generally overrated by students of Asian systems. However, when a boxer leads with his leg extended, a kicking attack to the knee can be a useful move, especially to close the distance.

I like to use elbow strikes with boxers because it confuses them for that split second before impact. They perceive the blow but realize something is wrong, then *bammo!* Also, since boxers are used to taking hard shots and don't give up too easily, I have found throws very useful to end battles, as throws are illegal in boxing but the clinch is part of the game.

Filipino Styles: Arnis, Escrima, Kali

To quote the Eagle, referring to his arnis instructor's opening talk about the Filipino arts: "Filipinos peaceful island peoples, but if have to fight, can do." It is recorded that Ferdinand Magellan, having circumnavigated the globe, was beaten to death by a Filipino arnis man with a ratan stick. Magellan, no doubt, was armed with a sword.

For you people who were sleeping during history class, Magellan was a Portuguese navigator of the 1600s who may have been the first person to sail around the

Earth. Unfortunately for old Ferdinand, this made him an invader when he got to the Philippines and met up with that arnis man with the stick.

The Filipino arts are much more directly designed for real fighting applications. They have not suffered much dilution by becoming modern sports. This is one reason why weapons, principally the knife and stick, are a big part of Filipino arts. There are others, of course, but these two are the ones I consider most useful.

Actually, stick fighting has been a sport in that part of the world for sometime. Only thing is, that sport often ended in the death of one or more of the contestants. The thing to understand is, learning how to beat the shit out of someone with a stick has some important relationships to learning how to effect same with just your hand. Besides, like the Eagle says, "Everything is a stick."

Learning how to wield a knife is a big help in seeing just how dangerous such a weapon is in the hands of a person who knows how to use it to some degree. This helps your defense against an actual blade attack. Arnis study will compel you to abandon all the classical martial arts approaches to knife defense because you will see how a blade is really used by a dangerous knifer.

These arts involve empty-hand techniques as well, but they may not be pretty like some people think a reverse spinning back kick is pretty. Nonetheless, they are brutal and effective if mastered. Arnis people have told me that they start out students with the stick before empty-hand techniques in order to teach perception of distance, focus, and evasive and continuous movement. This makes some sense to me.

Because of the emphasis on weapons, these arts also give you an edge when it comes to defending empty-handed against a knife or stick attack. Arnis is particularly strong in the disarm.

Another art I should mention is muay thai. If you happen to be in Southeast Asia, you can find a good instructor. This is an art for smaller, wiry, tough little monkeys. People are still killed in this sport as practiced in Asia. One of the things that sets this art apart is its use of the shin to strike the opponent in the ribs with sometimes devastating results. I sparred with a Thai kickboxer once and it was a painful affair for me, though my physical size was somewhat overpowering. He may have beaten me in a real fight with no rules, however. He struck me as a guy who had a lot of dirty tricks on hand for the actual battles. At that time I was much younger, faster, and stronger, too.

In addition, I think the Filipino arts are worth your study and attention if there is someone teaching them for real in your area.

The leading practitioners of the Filipino arts are generally considered to be Dan Inosanto and Remy Presas. "Hit one thousand times; is fantastic!"

DEALING WITH THE CROWD AND THE USE OF WEAPONS

I have been in fights with multiple opponents in the bar, but they didn't last too long before the other bouncers showed up. There was also a very brutal fight with some ambushers, but I have related that tale and there isn't much more to say except luck may have been as big a factor as skill in the outcome of that encounter. Mainly, I was lucky they didn't use knives.

Once I was in a "fight" with about twenty guys in a parking lot behind this jazz club where I was being paid to repossess some equipment that the band was packing up after the show. Like I said, I have some class; I waited until the performance was over before I started packing up their stuff.

I had some help on this repo job, all of whom promptly disappeared as soon as there was any sign of potential violence. Thus, your narrator was left facing about twenty guys in the parking lot. Once again, my luck held and I was able to bluff my way through by taking out two guys real fast and "projecting" on the crowd. Therefore, I didn't actually have to fight all those people.

My conclusion about defending against multiple attackers is that you aren't likely to do so with success. Therefore, refer to Chapter 1 on *avoidance*. Here is more advice, such as it may be worth on this subject.

First, if you are faced with a bunch of guys all moving around for position to attack, realize this and don't let them do it. You must go on the offensive; you can't afford anything else. Keep turning your gaze so that everybody is always in view and they know you see them.

There are two objectives in a quick attack on multiple opponents. One is to hurt some people right away to discourage the others while they are still thinking about whether or not or in what order they want to move on you. Seeing someone bleeding on the ground sometimes discourages the others because they really don't want that to happen to them, too. It also distracts people; they start looking at the guy on the ground or trying to help him up and such. This makes them less dangerous to you at the moment they are distracted.

Remember, for any one member of the crowd the whole scene is basically just entertainment, but for you it may be damn close to a fight for survival. This gives you a psychological edge, particularly when you make them know it. Spilling someone's blood goes a long way toward giving them the idea.

The second objective of such an attack is to drop somebody or stun them enough to make an opening and try to get away (be warned, though; I have never had to test this tactic in a real fight). If they pursue, you will at least have a chance to pick up a weapon like a stick or pipe. You might use a "reverse ambush" on the guy who catches up with you first, but do not spend too much time with any one guy. Keep moving. Escape is best, of course, and adrenaline will help. Keep your eyes open for that weapon. If you have studied some weapon arts that involve the use of the stick, this is when it could pay off. Not only will it increase your confidence, which is just about everything in this situation, but you have much less chance of being disarmed by the average Joe.

I'm sure no Remy Presas with the stick or jo, but if I get a good billy-club-type weapon in my hand (a snapped-off pool cue works well, particularly when it's snapped off over the first attacker's head), I'd feel pretty safe against two or three guys with just their bare hands. They generally don't want to get hurt and know they can after they see that first guy bite it hard. Also, I won't give them one second to think about it; I will take the fight directly to them, screaming and swinging that cue to reduce their able-bodied numbers even more should anyone stand between me and escape. Then I am out the door and gone. Even a hard stick shot to the elbow or wrist is very painful and can incapacitate someone for a moment at least.

In the parking lot with the twenty guys, I knew I was potentially in real trouble. Look, people, unless you have an automatic weapon or flamethrower, when you face more than two or three guys who are determined to get you, they will get you. This meant I had to reduce their determination by the preemptive strikes on the two closest guys.

This isn't much different from sucker punching, only they are the ones with their attention on you. This is where a good sliding-up advance is real handy on someone who thinks he is at a safe distance and believes he can react in time if you attack.

Keep in mind, this is a matter of perception. A guy backed up by a dozen or more other guys perceives that you will not attack him. Should you find yourself in a similar situation, be economical in your movement but otherwise make a show of it. Give them some screaming (*kiai!*) as you blast that guy. You want them to be startled and wonder what the hell is going on. You want them to think, "Who or *what* am I about to fuck with here?"

Working the crowd like this means controlling their determination to get you. This comes down to the price any individual in the mob is willing to pay to get you.

Guess what? Everybody is looking for a bargain. In my admittedly limited experience in dealing with a crowd, it seems everyone wants that first guy to engage you so they can safely move in and blindside you. Many of them are even going to wait for that second guy to blindside you and get you down so then they can move in for the stomp. You can't afford to let them get the ball rolling. This is the tactical rationale behind the preemptive strike. Don't wait for anyone to be the first guy to attack. Instead, you are the first guy to attack.

Letting Technology Do Some of the Work

The ideal way to discourage a group assault may be the use of a weapon. Suppose you pull a blade and look like a crazy man, jerking your head around, turning and moving as you face everyone and nobody, all the time yelling something like, "Come on! Who's first? Who wants to die first?" You may find that suddenly there seems to be no takers. If nobody wants to be the first to engage the knife, this can give you the time to escape.

On the other hand, when you pull the knife, somebody else may pull out a gun and shoot you in the belly. Like I said, there are no guarantees in a fight. Knife displays will often draw the police, however, which may be real timely for you if you're about to be beaten to death by a mob.

A stick can work, but you had better charge and drop a few people right away with some good, controlled shots to achieve the desired deterrence effect. Your arnis study could pay off handsomely in such a predicament.

But golly, where to find that stick in time?

I have found firearms to be an uncannily effective deterrent against a mob, but guns can cause severe legal problems. The charge will either be "felony menacing" or "illegal possession of a firearm." Take it from a man who knows (no conviction on either count). You'd better hope the charge doesn't become "voluntary manslaughter." Playing with guns makes this pretty easy to achieve, especially when combined with a little alcohol and some fear-based adrenaline.

If you have a gun, do not panic. Try to avoid shooting people or it's going to mean hard prison time almost for sure. But do not allow yourself to be disarmed by the crowd or someone may use the weapon on you.

Should the cops show up, put down the weapon, raise your hands above your head immediately, and yell, "Police! Help! Help!" Failure to do so at once may make you the target for multiple police bullets. I had an occasion to surrender to police after having had to display a gun to a crowd. Okay, the "crowd" only consisted of four guys, but it was a special circumstance.

Basically, I do not carry weapons as a rule because of the potential legal problems. Few situations will require them anyway. It's just that the ones that do may cost you your life if you are unarmed. I have decided to take my chances rather than risk the more likely legal jeopardy.

Things are different in my own home. I keep my friends Smith and Wesson among others quite handy. I sometimes carry a blade and always a stick in the car.

A few years ago I owned a liquor store. Maybe I should have called it Wild West Liquors considering the armed robberies that went down there. Needless to say, I lawfully carried a gun all the time then. Your humble author practiced with the weapon regularly and developed some measure of skill. Every time before I went to work, I would draw the weapon quickly to make sure it would clear my clothing smoothly.

Sound exciting? Well believe me, people, it was not. I was afraid I'd shoot the wrong guy on reflex as much, if not more, than I worried about not being fast enough to kill an armed robber. Luckily, things worked out for me on both those counts. I can't see how cops deal with this shit all the time without becoming paranoid freaks. Unfortunately, some cops do become paranoid freaks.

The liquor store was eventually sold, although not because of the gun play. Business in the area just really went to hell.

Keeping your head and knowing when *not* to go for your gun (like when the guy's already got the sawed-off shotgun leveled at your gut) is an important mind-set to maintain during a crisis involving firearms. It is at least as important as a fast draw and accurate shooting.

A lot of people carry knives on their belts. A few can draw one very fast and have some idea how to use it once they get it out. Unless you have a very good reason to carry a knife, I do not recommend it.

Some will say that they do have a good reason to carry that shank, namely staying alive! Well, keep in mind that if you're attacked with a blade, you won't have time to get yours out anyway, and while you are trying to get to yours, the guy will likely be cutting the piss out of you or killing you. Concentrate on the unarmed defense against the blade because that's all you will have time for in most real knife attacks.

This is true for cops who carry guns, too. A lot of cops have been stabbed to death because they were going for their gun rather than trying to grab and control the knife hand first. This is definitely one of those "first things first" deals. Grab his knife hand to keep the blade out of your guts, then maybe you will be around long enough to draw your gun and blow the bastard's brains out.

Lately I have taken to keeping an electronic stun gun handy. I have never had a reason to use it so I can't be sure it will work. However, I am pretty sure I could get it on a guy in most attack scenarios. The same skills used in blasting somebody with any of the natural tools I have talked about will apply directly to getting the stun-gun electrodes on his throat or groin. If I have to use the sucker, I hope the legal situation will be easier to deal with than if I used a stick, knife, gun, or just had to beat him into a bloody mess.

Do you see the advantage in simply trying to spot and avoid these problems in the first place?

A FINAL WORD

I opened this book with the observation that "anybody can get their ass kicked." This means me, and it almost certainly means you, too. If there really is such a thing as luck, then I guess I've had more than my share when it comes to dealing with violent encounters.

The more you train and practice, the quicker and stronger you become at evading a blow and returning a counterstrike, and the less you feel threatened by the challenge. The more experience you have with such senseless violence, the easier it is to see through the challenge or to spot the ambush beforehand.

It all leads to the same attitude: your attention turns to developing more effective avoidance techniques since you see that the battle is almost always avoidable if handled properly. Moreover, there is always more than a decent chance that you will get hurt even if you are "good." Either way, the legal system is one hell of a thing to have to deal with.

Above all, try to examine this "machismo madness" thing in yourself in as honest a manner as you are capable of. This is the only road to your controlling it rather than it controlling you. Now go back and read Chapter 1 again, and by the way, thanks for buying my book.